anna
mister god
and the black
knight

Also by Fynn
in Thorndike Large Print

Mister God, This is Anna

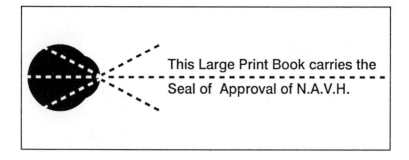

This Large Print Book carries the
Seal of Approval of N.A.V.H.

anna mister god and the black knight

The Long-Awaited Companion to
Mister God, This is Anna

FYNN

Illustrations by Papas

Thorndike Press • Thorndike, Maine

Library of Congress Cataloging in Publication Data:

Fynn.
 Anna, Mister God, and the Black Knight / Fynn.
  p.   cm.
 ISBN 1-56054-252-7 (alk. paper : lg. print)
 1. Anna. 2. Christian biography—England. 3. Large
type books. I. Title.
[BR1725.A73F96   1992]   91-29810
209'.2—dc20   CIP
[B]

Thorndike Press Large Print edition published in 1992
by arrangement with HarperCollins Publishers.

Cover illustrations by Papas.

The tree indicium is a trademark of Thorndike Press.

This book is printed on acid-free, high opacity paper.

anna
mister god
and the black
knight

Introduction

Fynn is, at heart, a teller of tales. Across the years I have come to think of him more and more as a "scop" (pronounced, I think shop), who in Early English times as a poet or minstrel would arrive in a village and immediately be surrounded by young and old beseeching him to tell them a story. The tale could be a slice of folk history or a fable. Often it would have some moral overtones. Of these the people would not always be aware. Neither, for that matter, would the scop. In any event we may be sure that it would be the tale and not the truth that held the spell.

Fynn is a born raconteur; he has a passion to *tell*. But he also has an equal and balancing passion: the passion to *know*. As this story clearly shows, from a very early age he yearned to know the way things were: how they worked, what was the cause, could it be other? And for him this spirit of enquiry, particularly mathematics, became a way of life. But, because he was never incorporated within the constraints of a profession at "school," he was always "on the way," off on an expedition to unexplored territory, not following a pilgrimage to a predetermined end. He was always open to, and constantly stumbling upon, almost, it seems by accident, new modes of knowledge and experience. And thus the quality which most accurately represents him is the capacity to wonder; to question, certainly, but at the same time to revere the world.

And yet, strangely, in conversation, and in his tales, there are many times when he would give the impression of being totally unaware of the element of transcendence hidden in the space between the words, as he speaks and writes about simple, ordinary things.

It was this trait, in my view, which made *Mister God, This is Anna,* his first book, such an immediate success with so many different kinds of people in so many different places. Conditioned by the media to having their imagination nourished by saga and story, they found a straightforward, and moving tale which threw up all sorts of other dimensions as well. At some levels Anna met a not-wholly-articulated need for light on human existence.

The story of *Anna, Mister God, and the Black Knight* was being lived, or "told," at the same time as the story of *Mister God, This is Anna;* the Black Knight was there, but not

8

in focus. In fact, one of the fascinating aspects of this tale is the way that Fynn shows that there is an infinite set of human stories inherent in a relatively small group of relationships. Alter the focus, move the centre, and see what happens. There is a sort of relativity in human relationships which is brought about by changing perspectives.

Now Fynn, may not for the most part, have to set out deliberately to reveal all these facets. They are part of the story's hidden "within." He does not regard his tasks as either to teach or to preach and the reader must guard against treating this book as an allegory, looking for arcane meanings in every episode. He is certainly not trying to score points for God at every corner. Certainly there are many seminal ideas latent in the experiments and the dialogue, but though the main theme celebrates — if that is the right word — the waning of one specific way of looking at the world, much of the book is straightforward narrative.

But is it true? It is true for Fynn. And it is as true as Fynn can make it.

The author of *Oranges Are Not the Only Kind of Fruit,* a TV series which centred on her strange, constricted, religious upbringing in a northern town, was asked how true the drama was. She replied that it was difficult

9

to say, because the memory manipulates fact and fiction and blurs the distinction between them. This is true for all of us. If you doubt it compare your memory of an episode in your childhood with that of a sibling! But it is particularly true of story-tellers who, albeit unconsciously, have to garnish, dress, elaborate, and work their tale into a particular "form." The Gospel writers were no exception.

However, Fynn is reaching back over almost fifty years, and through the condensing lens of his specific interests and personal concerns. Who could guarantee to remember accurately at that distance precisely who said what and where, and whether some lapidary truth put into the mouth of a character, is not a sentence read somewhere in the remote past, but registered then and remembered?

Undoubtedly Anna and The Black Knight *were* once on a day. But they are here recalled by Fynn in *his* way. Others would tell a different tale.

In any case, what is truth? Pilate asked the question long ago but, fearing the onslought of a series of philosophical abstractions, had the sense not to wait for a reply. Kierkegaard, faced with the same question, answered, "It is that which ennobles." A friend of mine, whilst discussing the ambiguity of all moral action, once asked Father Ronald Knox "How then *do* we know truth?" Knox thought for a long time, then said, "Truth . . . is that which makes you a better man."

Now read on.

VERNON SPROXTON

Anna and the Black Knight

Growing up in our little street meant only one thing — getting to the top of the railway wall. A red brick wall nearly ten feet high. Getting to the top of that wall was one thing all the boys wanted to do. It was then that you were grown up. Grown up enough to get a job and earn some money. Grown up enough to stay out late and have a girl friend of your own. It was almost like some sort of ceremony, attempting that wall. Everybody watched you and groaned in sympathy when you failed, which was most likely, and cheered on those very few occasions when somebody managed to get to the top and sit astride the wall. There were a number of ways to get to the top, like swinging from the lamp post to the top. It was not more than four or five feet away.

You could also climb out of Norman's top window. Anybody could do that. Of course, you could always "borrow" a ladder from the builder's yard but that wasn't growing up, that was just plain cheating. Our kind of growing up was something entirely different. It was simple really. Run as fast as you could for about sixty yards or so, jump as high as you could and hope that your speed and that last mad scramble would take you to the top. As there was nothing to hold on to until you reached the top the inevitable happened — you crashed to the ground! It was easy to see who had tried the wall that day — a bloody nose, a fresh bandage, a torn trouser. Such little things were reminders for all to see.

Getting to the top of that wall was one thing I was determined to do. I don't know how many times I had failed. I never kept count, but it was on such an occasion when I had landed with a crash from that wall that it happened. I know that my nose was bleeding a bit, so I sniffed. Bleeding noses didn't matter at all, as Mum so often said, it lets out the mad blood. Lying on my back I was aware of two people looking down at me. I had no idea who the lady was, but there was no mistake about the man. It was Old John D. Hodge himself.

I had heard a lot about Old John D. He was one of the Senior Masters at the posh school, but I had never seen him. Many people had described him to me and I didn't like him. Not one bit. He was slightly hunch-backed with a club-foot and a harelip which he kept covered with a large bushy beard. That sounded bad enough to me, but I was told

that he also carried around with him a length of bunsen burner tubing, which he used instead of a cane and which he had no hesitation in using when things didn't go to his liking, which from the sounds of things was often. The tubing was called the "persuader" by everybody. He was the stuff that nightmares were made of.

Looking down at me looking up at the sky, he laughed at me. He didn't realize how important this wall was. Nobody laughed at that. It was much too important to laugh at . . . I was going to have another try at it, and so I did, but the result was just the same. I failed and, as usual, ended up a heap on the floor.

"Only heroes never say 'No.' Neither do fools." He was still there and smiling down at me. No, I didn't like him. Not one little bit. I bet he couldn't climb that wall either. I was a bit fed up with that silent and quizzical look he gave me when I failed with the wall, and that slow shake of his head annoyed me. "Only heroes never say 'No.' Neither do fools." I just wished he would go away and leave me alone.

I was very surprised when the postman handed me that letter one morning. The one that said I had passed my examinations with good marks. I had got that scholarship and a small grant of money which was so important to me, and I could go to one of the posh schools. I didn't think that was going to happen. It was the Maths paper that was the problem. The first nineteen questions were so easy that I never bothered with them, but the last question was the one that interested me most of all, so I tried it. I didn't get very far with it. An hour's work left me a few pages of notes and lots of scribble, but no answer to the problem. I was a little comforted to be told some months later that nobody had ever attempted to answer that question before.

So there I was. All polished and dressed up in my nice new school uniform just off to catch the bus.

"Mum," I said, "what is the point of going to school to learn some more?"

"You've got to learn more," she replied, "to protect your self from what you already know," which is one of those sayings that takes you months to understand, but Mum always did have a way of turning things upside down. She had this odd way of putting things that left me standing on my head.

So it was that we all sat waiting for something to happen. I had managed to get the corner seat at the back of the classroom and soon we heard someone limping along the passage. We all held our breath as the door opened. There he stood, exactly as I had been told: Old John D. Hodge — our form-master!

"I will talk," he began, "and you will listen. Is that understood?"

We nodded.

"I will teach and you will learn. Right?"

Again we nodded.

"If any of you don't want to learn there is always another way of going about it," and he hit the desk with the "persuader."

"Who arranged the order for you to sit in?"

For the next few minutes we were all changing places until he was satisfied. I suddenly found myself at the front of the class. Somebody was detailed to hand out exercise books and we were told to write our name, form and address of the school on the cover of the exercise books and, like so many other pupils must have done, mine ended up with:

> London
> England
> Europe
> World
> Solar system
> Universe

I was sorry that I had done that when he began to walk around the room looking at our efforts. I did try to cover it up with my hand. And then his hand was under my chin as he tilted my head back.

"Well, well, young man, you certainly know where you are. I wonder, are you as certain where you are going. Are you?"

"No, sir," I replied. Perhaps it was at that moment that something happened. Suddenly I was looking into the bluest eyes I had ever seen. I tried to turn away but he held my head tight.

"You're the one that likes to climb things, aren't you?"

"Yes, sir."

"Ah, I think I can give you plenty of things to climb. Plenty! I can promise you that!"

The little street where I lived was a real rag-tag and bobtail of a place. Most of my friends lived here. The triplets were amongst our best friends and whenever the kids were playing in the street, it was pretty certain that if Bombom the black goddess wasn't looking after them, then I was.

The triplets were Millie's younger sisters. Their real names were Billie, Leslie and Josephine, but nobody ever called them that. We all called them Ready, Willing and Able. Something had happened to them. They were strange. I suppose modern medicine would be able to give whatever had happened to them a name. In those days some people simply called them daft or soft in the head. Perhaps now we might be more kindly and call them mentally handicapped. But if three kids could be truly called angels, it was Ready, Willing and Able. Without a husband their mother struggled hard to bring up five kids.

The little street was always very protective, and it was no rare sight to see one or other of the women bearing down on number 12 with some steaming left-overs from their own meals. None of the other kids were beyond snitching the odd cabbage, potatoes or, if they were lucky, an apple or two from the Market. PC Laithwaite was quite aware of these acts

of pilfering and, under May's leadership, many of the stall holders in the market place were always studiously looking somewhere else when the raiders were about. So all in all they didn't do too badly. After all, the alternative was the Workhouse and nobody in their right mind would wish that on anybody, not even their worst enemy. Things like money for the rentman, the coalman and the gas meter made things more difficult to deal with. Money was in very short supply down our street. On very rare occasions somebody had a few bob to spare and we all knew where that had to go.

So far as Millie was concerned there was only one thing to do and she did it. She joined the big house at the top of the street with the other girls. We all knew why Millie was "on the game" as it was called, but to begin with we had no idea why the rest of them were at it and certainly nobody was going to condemn them.

Danny and I had more fights over those girls than we ever did for our own pleasure. We were like a couple of knights even though our armour was fairly rusty, but woe betide anybody who said anything about the girls.

One of us would say, "It's my turn, you thumped the last one." Wallop. "That's another one who won't say that again." When

21

PC Laithwaite called on us with some complaint made at the local by some man who didn't understand what the situation was, all he asked was, "How many times did you hit him?"

"Once, of course, why? With this, of course," said Danny, holding up his fist. "What else?"

"Nothing, I suppose. Just wondered. Well, don't do it again then."

"Won't," said Danny, "it's Fynn's turn next."

Both of us had spent a night in the lock-up. Not that we were really locked up, because Danny had spent his time playing Twenty One with the sergeant. I spent mine reading *The Police Manual* and drinking tea. We were both home in time for breakfast. This fact about Millie and the girls up at the top was something that neither John nor Arabella — the spinster sister who lived with him — knew about and none of us was going to tell them. Eventually it was PC Laithwaite who told them. I'm sorry to say that they understood much better than the Rev. Castle did. Maybe he was just too concentrated on souls, but he needn't have worried because Danny and I had fixed them up with a place to pray in, and even though the Vicar had said an altar was out of the question. Well, the flowers were "by courtesy" of the local park.

I don't know when, or how, I came to like John D. I never thought I would, but it wasn't all that long before I found it a real pleasure to be with him. It could have been — possibly — that as my father had died so long ago old John was coming to be important to me. Whatever the reason might be, it always gave me great pleasure being with him, even though he always seemed to be having a dig at me in one way or another. I know that I had never met anyone like him before. He could hardly utter a sentence without being sarcastic, but his dry manner of giving a lesson was something that excited me. I just liked listening to him. Even the dreaded "persuader" didn't bother me. It didn't hurt all that much, and after a minute or two it was as if nothing had happened at all.

I was just about to make my way home from school when he called me over to his car and first introduced me to his sister Arabella.

"One of your friends has just changed the tyre for my sister," he said.

"I wonder who that was," I began to say.

"His name was Danny Sullivan."

"Good old Danny! He's my fighting mate."

"So," he continued, "you are the one they call Fynn, are you? I've heard about you. I understand you have other things you like doing. Other than fighting and climbing impossible walls."

I nodded.

"And may one ask what else young Fynn likes doing?"

"Mathematics mostly. I guess I like that most of all."

"The art of the mind."

"What?" I asked. "I don't understand that."

"The art of the mind," he said once again. "Mathematics."

That idea was a new one on me.

"Have you many books on the subject?" he asked me.

"Not many," I said, "they are all falling to bits and I reckon they are a bit out of date now."

"Maybe. If you would care to come to my study after school is over, I'll see if I can find anything for you. We mustn't let our finest brains suffer from lack of books, must we?" The sarcastic old so and so!

"Who knows," he went on, "we may even manage to kindle some spark in that head of yours, but please keep it away from walls until I am able to see if there is anything inside! I doubt it. I doubt it very much, but it is just possible!"

The next day after school had ended I went

to his study. Away from the classroom he was a different person altogether. He was still dry, sarcastic as ever and never missed any opportunity to trip me up, but he asked me many questions. He handed me a bundle of books.

"Here you are, young Fynn, see what you make of these. I don't suppose you'll make much of them, but you never know. What will you do, young Fynn, if you don't understand them?"

"Try to work it out, I suppose. I don't know yet."

"You could always come and ask me if you get stuck. Come after school. I'm always ready to help you out. We really can't afford to let the spark go out now, can we? That's if we ever manage to kindle it."

I smiled and he turned his back on me.

John had had a very bad time of it in the 1914–1918 War and would rarely speak of it. What with that experience and the deformities that he had been born with, he had become slightly sour. The very mention of the word "God" or "religion" often provoked an outburst of scorn and anger. He was that strangest of mixtures of outspoken bitterness and almost total generosity. I really had to be so careful with him and choose my words with great care.

It was one of his great pleasures to be called a rationalist and, after World War I, Arabella and he had joined a new group called The New Liberation Society. From the little that I knew of it, I knew it was not for me. Even though in those days I did like a tight argument it appeared to me that the rationalists were carrying things a bit too far.

The whole of John's personal life was so strictly regimented and his possessions so carefully ordered that no room was left for any kind of spontaneous gesture. If a thing could not be calculated it more or less did not exist for him, so much of a rationalist was he.

On the other hand, he could be very kind. He was more than willing to help those of his students who found it hard to grasp the point, and his willingness to help old comrades who had suffered in the war knew no bounds. On those occasions he was all gentleness and concern. He was an odd mixture, and the mix made it difficult for some people to understand him.

It must have been late summer or so when I had gone to see Old John to ask him for help. I was completely stuck with a problem. Although I had tried all the various ways that looked possible, I was just unable to resolve it. He looked at the problem for a moment or two, pointed out my mistake and left me to it. Of course, it was such a silly mistake to have made. The resolution of it was so simple that I could have kicked myself. He edged his way through the door from the kitchen, bearing a tray of coffee and some buns.

"Solved it, young Fynn?"

I nodded. "I feel a right fool. How did I ever come to make that mistake?"

"It's one of the hazards of mathematics, Fynn!" He laughed. "It so often turns out to be the simple thing. I've done it often myself."

It gave me a lot of comfort to hear that. He handed me a cup of coffee and asked, "Well, young Fynn, your sentence is almost up. Any idea what you are going to do with yourself?"

It was true. I was of an age when earning a living was necessary. I had one or two ideas, but I hadn't made up my mind.

"Well, what might my young genius do?"

"Not really sure yet, John," I replied. "Just don't know. All I am certain of is that I can't give up mathematics or physics."

"Glad to hear you say that, young Fynn. You're always welcome here, you know that. But what about earning your keep, eh? An accountant? A teacher? There's plenty of room in this world for anyone able to add two and two together."

"I know that, John, but I don't think that I want to do that sort of thing."

"Why is that?" he asked.

"I know it sounds a bit daft, John, but I enjoy it too much! I suppose I just don't want to lose the fun and magic of it."

His laughter at that filled the room. "Oh, Fynn, oh Fynn, I've always known that to be a fact. You are reasonably good at it, you know, even if occasionally you do some silly things. That makes you doubly welcome here. Have you no idea what you might do then?"

This was the question I dreaded most of all, but the time had come to answer it.

"John . . . well . . . I . . . I, er . . . think I would like to go into the Church."

I waited for the explosion, but it never came. He merely said "Oh," and his voice dropped a couple of octaves. Still there was no explosion, no tirade against religion. Just a simple, "Why, Fynn? Why? Can you tell me?"

"It's just important, John, that's all, I can't give you any more reason than that."

"Important, certainly," he replied. "Important to know where we are, and why too, if that's a proper question. I'm really not certain of that."

His calmness had left me totally puzzled. "John, I thought that you would . . ."

"I would blow my top . . ."

I nodded.

"You know, Fynn," he said with a smile, "I wasn't born without faith. I had to work very hard for my lack of it. I wouldn't want to stop you becoming a priest, if that is what you really want. All I must ask of you is that you think hard and long before you make up your mind."

Perhaps I had made some movement, some indication that I was about to ask a question. He laid his hand on mine.

"No questions, young Fynn, not now. Perhaps one day when you visit me, and I am sure that there will be many days, many, many visits, I might even tell you all, but not now. There is one thing, however, that bothers me most of all, which you might like to ponder over before you take the plunge. Will you please fetch my Bible from my study? It's on the small table by the lamp. Don't look so surprised, Fynn. I really do have a Bible, and what is more I have even read it. In fact, more than once, mainly in the hope that I might have missed something, but I fear I haven't."

I fetched the Bible and put it on the chair beside him and waited. His next words were such a surprise that I had to laugh.

"Do you drink beer, Fynn?"

"Well, I have once or twice, not much though."

"Perhaps a small glass won't hurt a young man who is soon to go into the world. It's my own brew and I'm really rather proud of it." He handed me a glass of beer.

"Before you drink perhaps you will read me verses 19 and 20 of the second chapter of Genesis."

"And out of the ground the Lord God formed every beast of the field and every fowl of the air, and brought them unto Adam to see what he would call them and whatsoever Adam called every living thing that was the name thereof. And Adam . . ."

"Enough, enough," John broke in. "Now you may drink."

I took a swig.

"Well, what do you think of that?"

"Think of what?"

"The beer first, of course, and if you have any comments, the verses next."

"The beer is good, John."

"Good, Fynn? Good? Why, the only word to describe that beer is sublime. Take another draught and then tell me what you think about those verses."

"I can't see anything wrong with them, John. They look all right to me. If they are true, it's wonderful. What are you on about?"

"I'm not on about anything. If, as we are told, God is all powerful, omnipotent, etcetera, etcetera, then why, oh why am I required to be amazed, pleased or full of wonder at the things he is supposed to have made? I'm not. What does puzzle me, however, is why then did he do such a stupid thing as to ask Adam to name them? Damn it, Fynn. I mean Babel and all that nonsense. What with that and the supposed flood, he does seem to me to spend a lot of time undoing his own creations. If only Adam had had the good sense to give everything a number rather than a name, it would have saved us all a lot of heartache. Ah well, my young friend, after too many years of trying to teach mathematics, I have come to the conclusion that it's the 'numb' in numbers that causes the blockage. That is partly the reason why I am always so happy to have taught you and will always be so glad to see you. You are just a tiny bit different from my other pupils. Not much, mind you, but enough!"

I wanted to say something that would justify my difference, but nothing came.

"For goodness sake, Fynn, don't look so dumbfounded. Finish off your drink and indulge me occasionally in my hobby-horses. My problem is really quite simple. I cannot believe. It's as simple as that. If I could, I would, but even now I have not said what I wanted to say. Anno Domini, I suppose. What I am trying to say to you is, whatever else mathematics might be, it is certainly a language and that's important. Now, my young friend, it's about time you were off. Let me know what you decide to do and please come again and often."

I was really quite confused by all this. He had never been as open with me before and I felt that I would like to stay with him, except that it wouldn't have been much use because I was perhaps even more uncertain about things myself. The idea that mathematics was a language was new to me and it gave me much to think about, for if it was true that you could talk about God in any language and if mathematics was a language, then . . . except that I couldn't see how that might work.

I never did become a priest. I just wasn't sure enough for that. I became involved in the blending of oils and all sorts of lubricants. I suppose it was interesting enough. At least I was earning a wage, but except for adding a few numbers now and again and the occasional need to find seven per cent of a barrel of oil containing forty-seven gallons, my knowledge of maths was rarely used. It wasn't much used in conversation either. If I said that a particular problem and its solution was very beautiful, I found I had produced one of the best conversation-stoppers.

Fortunately, mathematics does have one great advantage. You don't need much to do it with — paper and pencil, perhaps, but often not even that. In fact, nothing but the room and time in which to think. So my roaming around the docklands of London at night were times of great contentment. I might meet the odd cat or two, perhaps a seaman overfilled with beer, trying to find his ship, or those ladies who called me "Dearie," but whether it was cats, tarts or drunks, the well-aimed answer "Pi R squared to you" or perhaps, "the square root of minus 1" was a sure-fire way of clearing a space!

Occasionally I met the dockland tapper or PC Laithwaite. Then one particular night when my head was full of numbers, Old John, God, language problems and all the odd bits and pieces of puzzlement, out of the fog a small girl suddenly appeared.

There was not much I could see of her in the fog even by a gas lamp. She was not very tall. She told me she had "runned away" and she carried an old rag doll, a box of paints and she was hungry. She made a large hole in my bag of saveloys and she liked fizzy drinks, particularly the ones with a marble in the neck.

A couple of necessary fags to regain my composure and I learned that her name was Anna, that she was going to live with me and that she loved me as I loved her. I never was one to get into an argument that I had no hope of winning, so I simply accepted all that she had told me.

As time went by I did try to find out more about her background, but nobody had missed her, or if they had, they did not want her back. So she came home with me and stayed until she died a few years later. Later that night a hot bath revealed a mop of fiery red hair and a number of bruises. As a hot bath revealed her own special beauty, so warm love laid bare her devotion to Mister God, her endless chatter and her enormous appetite for trying to find out about things, as I have described in *Mister God This is Anna*. I did try to keep Anna and John apart, but since I talked about them so much, it was inevitable that they would meet, and it made me nervous. Like keeping the positive and negative poles of a battery apart. If you do that, nothing happens. But then if you join the poles of a battery to various things, you might get anything from light to a blown fuse. Whatever it was that did happen between them I was always in the middle of it!

And so I was talking to John about taking Anna to church. "Church," he exploded, "utter piffle!" After his calm comments about my possibly becoming a priest, this outburst astonished me. But John liked to be perverse at times.

"Religion is nothing more than a bloody

fortress of chaos," he went on. "Haven't you yet learned that people will protect their wrong beliefs with greater ferocity than they ever will their right beliefs. I really cannot see how anybody can believe anything that cannot be proved."

"What about love, John?"

"What about it?"

"What about it! You can't prove that love exists!!"

"Indeed, what about it? What, may I ask, what good does that do?"

I said I didn't know but felt it must do some good.

These sudden outbursts never lasted very long, however, and were so quickly relieved by that crooked smile that his harelip forced upon him, but these sudden changes meant that we all had to be very careful what we said. He, himself, was very aware of these sudden outbursts, and that it made him a very lonely person; but for a long time it seemed that there was very little he could do about it. I suppose it accounted for the fact that he was so happy to give me as much extra tuition as I liked. I also think that he liked me. That pleased me.

John's manner of teaching was unusual; not odd, but different. On the occasions when he'd written some complex problem on the blackboard, he would always write out the answer on the board as well.

"Now you all know the answer, so you now all have ten marks. There are another ten marks for anyone who can tell me why it is right." And after writing the proof, he would always end up with the letters written large Q.E.D. or Q.E.F., whatever was appropriate. What seemed to give him the most pleasure was the final full stop done with vigour, almost as if he was attacking the blackboard. Turning to his pupils he would always utter the one word. "There!"

Listening to John delivering his lectures was not everybody's cup of tea, but his dry and precise manner of delivery was something I enjoyed greatly in spite of that slightly acidic way he had of going about it. Following his manner, I had also got into the habit of ending what I had written with Q.E.D. or Q.E.F.

When Anna first saw these letters she wanted to know what they meant and I showed her where to look in the Abbreviations section of the dictionary. She found another group that I did not know — Q.E.I., "that which was to be found." So now I had three sets.
1. Quod Erat Demonstrandum,
2. Quod Erat Faciendum, and

3. Quod Erat Inveniendum.

Q.E.D., "which was to be proved," and certainly John's pleasure;

Q.E.F., "which was to be done," and seemed always to be my job;

And Q.E.I., "which was to be found," and Anna's main delight.

"Squashed-up writing" was what Anna called abbreviations. And for her mathematics was simply "All squashed-up writing."

Sometimes it was difficult to understand what Anna was saying. Her invented words took some getting used to. Once, in a moment of pride, I took some pages of her writing to show John D., eager to hear what he would say about them. I was angry when, a few days later, I collected them, and found that he, apparently tripped up by her "talk," had simply corrected the grammar and spelling in red ink. She was never very good at spelling or grammar. She had her own way.

Anna had been with me when John had launched himself into his usual anger about religion. "If there was just one religion," he said, "I might be tempted to study it, but there are so many of them it's as if everybody has their own God and *that,* Fynn, is really beyond me. If there is an answer, there can only be one."

Anna had written down her own solution

to this problem but John hadn't grasped it. He had simply busied himself with corrections.

"It's easy, Fynn," she had said. "One of the first things Mister God ever did do was when he made light, wasn't it?"

"Agreed. That's what it says."

And then she reminded me of the thing we had done together when, with the aid of a prism, and a beam of light, we had made that little spectrum of light on the wall. That's what it was all about. "The Catholics used the red colour, the Protestants used green, the Jewish people another colour, the Hindu people yet another colour to see Mister God by." Of course there were lots of different religions, and Anna was never really certain that somebody might not suddenly find another with one more holy day to cut out of the week, so that she would have less time than ever to play with her friends. But it didn't really matter when you saw them all as beams of the one light. As Mum said, you are born into one religion because you have no choice, but you die with them all or nothing. John very nearly missed this other way of looking.

Anna's times at School or Church didn't always achieve those aims intended by Miss

Haynes or the Rev. Castle. For that matter, John also came in for a good few "Poohs." Some of all this teaching was not bad, but some of it was just downright "daft, wasn't it, Fynn?" Poor old Rev. Castle most definitely was not pleased one bit to be so loudly "Poohed" in the middle of his sermon, and the way he had peered at me over his spectacles made it look as if it was my fault. I did try to keep her quiet, but it never worked all that well. The Vicar had been telling

the congregation the parable about the sower sowing the seeds. The fact that some of them fell among stones and others fell among thorns was a little bit too much for her. Her "Pooh!" was startling enough, but her comment that he ought to be more careful was so loud that I'm sure even the statues heard it. It didn't help matters afterwards when she was heard telling me that this sower bloke was also a bit daft.

"He should have taken them stones out first. At least he should have dug them thorn things out, shouldn't he Fynn?" She almost convinced herself that the reason why grown-ups read fairy stories to children was because they, themselves, believed them!

I often taught Anna some of the things that John had taught me. She never was what you might call brilliant at mathematics, but she so often saw in it things that neither John nor I had seen, or at least not in the same way. For instance, multiplying two numbers together was fine if that was what you wanted to do. A bit of a bore at times and at times pretty hard to do. It was a great excitement for her when I showed her that 8 times 9 equals 72 was only one way of doing it. You got exactly the same result by dividing one number by the reciprocal of the other. The idea that you could "do" multiplication by division was for me such an absurd idea that it just stuck with me. Of course, it was one of those things I had to teach Anna.

She did change the words a bit. 9 or $9/1$ became "standing up" numbers and the reciprocal of 9 or $1/9$ was obviously "upside down" numbers.

It made much more fun for Anna to do her sums with this wonderful new way. The old stuff of multiplying 9 by 8 suddenly became either $9 \div 1/8$ or $8 \div 1/9$. It didn't matter which way you did it, it didn't make any difference to the answer. Whichever way you did it, the answer was always 72 and it was "the right way up" too. That certainly needed some thinking about.

$$8 \times 9 = 72$$
$$8 \div 1/9 = 72$$
$$9 \div {}^1/8 = 72$$
$$\frac{1}{{}^1/9 \times {}^1/8} = 72$$

I don't remember if I had ever thought of what happens if you multiply $1/9$ by $1/8$, but Anna did.

"What happens, Fynn, what happens if you make them both 'upside down' numbers and multiply them? $1/8 + 1/9 = \ldots$? What happens, Fynn, what happens?"

The fact that it turned out to be a 0.013888888 was a bit of a disappointment to her after this new and wonderful way of doing it.

I waited for her next question. It took a long time coming, but eventually it came. Suddenly she launched both herself and her question at me.

"Is it, Fynn? Is it?"

"Is it what, Tich?"

"Is it an 'upside down' number, Fynn, is it, eh?"

It was indeed a reciprocal or "upside down" number of 72 ($^1/_{72}$ = 0.013888888).

"Oooh! Fynn," she gasped, "ain't it good? Oooh! I'm going to tell Mister John next time. Do you think he knows about it, Fynn?"

"I reckon he does," I replied, "you can tell him about it tomorrow when we see him."

John chuckled with amusement and delight at her "right way up" and "upside down" numbers. He had never heard them called that before.

"I don't suppose it really matters what she calls them, as long as she knows what it means."

I left them to it for a few minutes. Anna was chattering away as fast as she could, and John was in his favourite armchair with a dazed but happy smile on his face. When I came back I heard him say, "Yes, my little maid, I'll remember, I will be careful."

"What was all that about, John?" I asked.

He laughed. "She just told me that sometimes the answer is 'upside down' and that makes a difference and you've got to remember what you've done." He poured himself a fresh tankard of ale. "I never remember being so excited about reciprocals in my education. Perhaps, young Fynn, it's the names she give things that I find so enchanting. 'Upside down numbers' indeed! That does seem to fit so many occasions and situations, don't you think?"

"Think, John? I don't often get the chance to think when she gets started!"

"The answer might be 'upside down,' " he muttered. "It so often is! Remember that, Fynn. The answer is sometimes 'upside down,' "

"Yes, John, I will. Sometimes I think it's me that is 'upside down'!"

"Ah!" He laughed. "She certainly does give it a new life, doesn't she?"

It didn't matter which way round you did it, the idea that it was possible to multiply by dividing and divide by multiplying was something entirely new to Anna. This must surely be real Mister God stuff. And then there was those logarithm things where you could multiply by adding certain kinds of numbers and divide by taking away certain kinds of numbers. John didn't see this magic as Anna saw it.

"You can do things like multiplication the ordinary way, you can do it by dividing and you can also do it by adding!"

That really was something to reckon with. So she plunged into mathematics with rare excitement. She never really did get into that Q.E.D. stuff. Proofs for her were a complete waste of time. There really was so much to find out.

After their first few meetings John had viewed her with tolerant amusement.

"She is so ignorant of the task ahead of her that she can't see the certainty of failure," he had said. He was just plain puzzled by her. It was much later that he said, "Well, I don't really know, whatever else might be said about her, she certainly does appear to proceed in a step by step fashion, even though I can't always follow her path!"

It was at this time that a curious magic happened between us: the "which was to be proved" retired school master, the "which was to be found" red-headed child, leaving me with the "which was to be done" bit as usual; but that was all right. It was worth it! It was always a great pleasure to see these two together. John slowly became much more relaxed about things, and after a time he was even capable of playing pretend games, even though he never was able to stop being the academic. Being with these two didn't do me any harm either, even though I did get myself into a muddle at times. After all, I could ask, couldn't I? And I often needed to. I wasn't always sure about the answer, but I never went without one.

It didn't take John too long before he could empty all the contempt from the word "brat" and fill it with love, in the way that Anna was able to empty the word "sir" from its association and fill it with love. Neither of them, however, was able to get out of their own way of speaking. John often threw in a foreign phrase or two and Anna's choice of words was not always of the best. But "brat" and "sir" they became to each other for a long time and, for the most part, I was able to translate the one to the other.

On the occasions when there was nobody around to see it, John would often wear the red-beaded heart that Anna had made for his birthday. Making brooches was not a thing that John would ever attempt to do, and it was some long time before he gave her one she kept for very special occasions. John had chosen a plain little silver brooch for her on which he had had inscribed some words in Latin; of course, what else! QUOD PETIS HIC EST.

Anna would never tell anybody what it meant when asked. "Ask Fynn. He knows."

I did like saying, "It means 'What you seek is hard'."

At one time I thought of having one made for her myself, just to keep the whole thing in order so to speak. Mine would have been different, like QUANTUM SUFFICIT — "As much as is sufficient." If only I had known exactly how much! But I never did find the answer to that one.

The fact that much of my time was spent with books on mathematics, physics and related subjects, meant that Anna picked up a number of unfamiliar words, like "electrons," "polynomials," "relativity" and "quantum theory." The fact that I never kept my books from her meant that she soon had words in her vocabulary which most people had never heard of or, if they had heard of them, didn't understand. Neither did she for the most part, at least, not in the way that would have allowed her to pass an examination. She simply sprinkled them about like salt and sugar. It didn't matter if the salt was where the sugar should have been. As a matter of fact I did not know all that much about them myself. But these words, in Anna's view, were the result of finding, and finding was to her all-important. A question mark was an invitation to finding. When she saw a chapter-heading IS THE ELECTRON DIVISIBLE ALSO?, she knew it was important. When the author went on to say, "Perhaps it is merely a co-incidence that the person who first noticed that the rubbing of amber would induce a new and remarkable state now known as the state of electrification was also some great unifying principle that links everything to-gether," she realized he was a friend of Mister God, and she was quite certain that it was Mister God who made it all happen.

"Any mathematical book to be of any value has to be read forwards and backwards." Nothing could be simpler, could it? So she tried it. It was something that was so simple to say and almost impossible to do, but in her own way she was often able to find some little gem out of the wreckage of instructions. She tackled this reading the book backwards idea with enthusiasm, even though to begin with she did think it was daft. It was easy for her to see that the best way to go about this thing was to prop a mirror on the kitchen table and read the reflection of the book in the mirror, not the book itself. It did seem to her to be a little bit like Mister God. After all, the Vicar never lost any opportunity to remind us that we could never actually see God, so the reflection was all that we had to go on. Mind you, it did mean that you had to be a bit careful!

I think that this was why she was so very interested in everything about her. For a few days I often saw her looking into the mirror, screwing her head to left and right. On my return from work one evening it was quite obvious that she was just ready to explode with excitement. The mirror was carefully set upon the table as she dived into her own private drawer and brought out a sheet of paper. It didn't seem to be all that important to me. She had simply written in large numbers 4 + 7 = 11.

"So, what's all the excitement about," I wondered. "That's pretty obvious stuff."

"So what?" I asked her. "What's that in aid of?"

"That's right, ain't it, Fynn?"

"Of course it is," I replied. "You know that. You didn't need to ask me."

"Look," she said. "Look now." She had turned the sheet of paper to face the mirror. The reflection now read $11 = 7 + 4$.

"That's right too," I said before she had a chance to ask me.

"Um," she said, "but, Fynn, what else is eleven equal to?"

"Well, it could be $10 + 1$ or $9 + 2$, it could be . . ."

She interrupted me with, "Couldn't it be squillions of things?"

"Yes, it could, couldn't it?"

"Fynn, that equals thing makes it safe, don't it?"

"Safe for what?" I asked, getting a bit lost as usual.

"Safe so you can read it backwards like Mister God."

Now I was completely lost. "How come like Mister God?" What was so clear to her left me a wee bit in the dark.

"Fynn," she replied with some exasperation, " 'cos if there is only one way to go frontways to see Mister God and he won't let us and there is squillions of ways of going backwards, what then?"

There was not much glimmer of light, but enough for the moment. Doing something backwards and forwards might seem odd at times, but sometimes it did work and then well, who knows, things might happen. I liked the idea that the = sign made it quite safe to go forwards or backwards, but I had never really grasped the fact that, of course, $4 + 7 = 11$ was, according to her, only right once when she read it forwards, but that there were squillions of answers when you read it backwards. $11 = 7 + 4$ or $8 + 3$ or ... or ... I was having enough trouble doing it the right way round! And I suppose Mister God just might have made it so that we couldn't see him frontwards in only one possible way, but that we had to look at him backwards like the reflection in a mirror. It did mean, as she told me, that there were simply squillions of ways to do it and that Mister God was in each way, and considering the fact that the little thing made it all so safe, that was fine.

"You'd better tell the Vicar," I said, "I'm sure *he'd* like to know." She wasn't all that certain about that!

"I'm going to tell Mister John the next time I see him. Bet he wants to know, Fynn, bet he do!"

Over the next few days she did manage to tell this to the Rev. Castle and, for that matter, anyone else who would listen. The Rev. Castle had responded, "There is absolutely no need for that kind of stuff in church, you know."

53

She got a great deal more response from the milkman and the coalman and Bombom and Millie, but that was all right. In the next few days most of the railway wall was filled with little sums as she and her friends explored this idea. It didn't look like Mister God to me, but, according to Anna, it was, just the same.

It was after this that the whole idea of mathematics made sense to her and she plunged into my books with some urgency.

Her way of doing things often got me into hot water; like the time we had been turned out of St Paul's Cathedral. She couldn't understand how we were "desecrating God's Holy Place." After all, we were just pushing a prayer book around the black and white squares on the floor, and what was the harm in that? It's true that we had written some numbers in chalk on the floor, but as she pointed out, "Fynn can get it off with his hanky," so why were we being turned out? This was God-stuff after all, wasn't it?

I was curious, considering the fact that John D. regarded the Bible as not worth reading as it was nothing more than a collection of fairy-stories, that he should be so offended when Anna could so easily laugh at it. The Rev. Castle was even more put out. His word for Anna's laughter was that she was making a mockery of it and that really I ought to do something about it. For both of them Life was a very serious business. Everybody said how hard Life was. It was odd that two people so far apart in their beliefs should think of God in the same way.

"People get muddled up," she told me.

"They must do," I agreed, "but about what?"

"Mister God and Old Nick."

"Oh, do they? How do they manage to do that? I can't see how they make that mistake."

"In church the Rev. Castle keeps on saying that Mister God is always looking at me."

"So, what's wrong with that?"

"I know that!"

"So?"

"Why does he say that Mister God stick me with a big sticker if I don't sit up straight and if I talk sometimes."

"Suppose other people want to hear what he's got to say and that children ought to behave themselves."

"Suppose so!" But obviously she didn't believe that was true. She tried to find the right words to explain to me what she was wanting to say, words that I could understand.

"I do try, Fynn, I really do."

"Try to do what, Tich?"

"Try to behave good, and sit up straight, and things like that."

"I know that."

"But I don't always, do I, Fynn?"

"Not always," I said, "sometimes you are a blessed nuisance, but I love you!"

She nodded and smiled at me. "So does Mister God too, don't he, Fynn?"

"Sure thing! I don't see how he could help it."

"It's them bloody stones, Fynn. They get heavy. That's what they are like, *stones.*"

"What stones are you on about, Tich? What kind of stones?"

"All the things they tell you to do. *Them*

kind of stones. That's what! And then they get so heavy, I can't do nothing. Mister God don't do that, do he Fynn?"

I was beginning to get the hang of this stones stuff. The Vicar was certainly full of "do's" and "don't's" and at times they did seem like heavy weights.

"It makes me laugh sometimes. It's funny!"

"Can't see what's funny about it. How do you work that one out?"

" 'Cos I can't do it. It's funny. I can't help laughing then, Fynn."

All this did sound complicated to listen to, but as far as I could see she wasn't far out.

The trouble with people like the Rev. Castle and John was that life was a deadly serious business, and so often they would load you up with dead weights and you certainly couldn't run and play. "If you had to carry all them stones around with you! Mister God never did mean you to do that kind of thing, did he?"

As far as Anna understood Mister God, he never went around prodding people to make them fed up or frightened of him. What Mister God really wanted was to make you laugh — to laugh at your own mistakes. If you could do that, you really did learn and did not get tangled up in things you couldn't possibly do. "It makes you laugh, don't it?"

*   *   *

It was about the middle of Autumn and I was just coming home from work. As I passed the Corner Shop I was hailed by Mrs Bartlett, our local shopkeeper, who, amongst other things, acted as a clearing house for telephone calls for those of us who had not as yet got a telephone. That meant all of us.

"Fynn," she called. "Got a message for you. The Professor's sister rang up this afternoon. The old chap's been taken bad and would you go as soon as possible?"

"Thanks, Missus," I said, "I'll get there as soon as possible after I've washed up a bit."

"Hope he's all right. He's a funny old geezer right enough. Meself, I can't understand what he's on about half the time. He ought to learn to speak English proper. That's what he ought to do." She chortled her next sentence, "How do you fancy me as a Madam, Fynn?"

"Well, I don't quite see it myself, but you never know!"

"That's what the old gent called me. 'Good afternoon, madam, have you by any chance got some French mustard?' And me with me curlers still in. 'Madam' indeed! It made me feel a right fool, it did!"

Mum was never ever surprised at my comings and going. As far as I was concerned, there wasn't all that difference between day and night.

"Have you told Anna yet?"

"No," I replied, "I haven't seen her yet."

"She went over with Bombom to May's house. I'll just tell her you had to go out. It's better not to say too much until you get home. Maybe it'll turn out to be nothing much after all. You can wake me up if you get home late. I'd like to know myself how the old fella is." I promised that I would do that as soon as I got in.

Now Random Cottage, where John and Arabella lived, was various distances away, depending on the route you took and, of course, what means of transport you could use where. Trams and buses took a long time. But I had worked out a route using the canal tow-path and other short cuts.

As I rode along my mind was working nineteen to the dozen. J. D. was, after all, no chicken and well, maybe . . . I didn't waste my time in getting there. I just pedalled as hard and as fast as I could. There was nothing out of the ordinary that I could see as I made my way to the back door. Arabella was doing something in the kitchen. I rang the bell and waited. She greeted me warmly.

"Hello, Fynn. Hope I didn't give you too

much of a scare. Thank you for coming so promptly. Go through to the study. John's there."

I breathed a sigh of relief for nothing at all seemed to be wrong. It was, as far as I could see, much the same as usual. John was in his usual chair with his usual pint of beer.

"Hello, young Fynn. Pour yourself a pint of beer and sit down. Don't look at me like that," he chuckled. "You look as if you've seen a ghost. Drink up. Well, as a matter of fact, I did have a bad turn, but, as you see, I'm fit as a flea now."

I was relieved to hear it and said so!

"I'm afraid, Fynn, that Arabella does get a little worked up about things, but there you are."

It was just like John to think that some people got worked up about unimportant things. I did wonder, for a moment of two, whether I ought to say what was in my thoughts and decided that I must. "You really must look after yourself."

"No, no, Fynn," he interrupted me, "don't you start on me. You are far too young to tell me what I must or must not do."

"Sorry," I replied. "You would not say that to Anna, would you?"

"That's an entirely different thing," he said. "You are beginning to think like me, so I feel free to correct you. Anna," he continued, "is far too young to want to offer me any advice. She has her own particular way of thinking and I do find what she says to be of some interest, even though I don't always understand what it is that she means."

That I was beginning to think like him, I

took to be a rare compliment, but it did seem odd to me that if I was more and more like him, why was it that he paid me so little attention or why was it that he was so interested in Anna's way of putting things?

"I had hoped," he said, "that you would have brought her with you. Didn't you think of that?"

"Of course I did," I replied with a touch of anger, "but I thought Arabella's telephone call sounded so urgent that you must be ill and, well . . ." I was stumbling over my words.

"Pooh!" he chuckled, "pooh and pooh again. You see, Fynn, it's never too late to learn."

I was hurt by his remarks. "If your being unwell is a pooh thing, I . . ."

"Sorry, Fynn, forgive me."

"There's nothing to forgive," I muttered.

"I'm very glad you came. I did want to see you. I have been giving something a great deal of thought these last few days and I wanted to talk to you about the matter."

I was very relieved at this. It sounded to me that he was back to his old self again, but I was totally unprepared for what he said next.

"Wouldn't it be nice if Anna could stay at Random Cottage for, say, a day or two?"

I was so totally surprised at this that I was quite unable to think of an answer.

"You look surprised, Fynn."

"A bit," I said.

"You know, I'm not the monster you take me to be. I too have a heart. The little one has never been frightened of me and that I find very pleasing."

He did seem disappointed when I told him that I couldn't possibly give him an answer right then and that I would have to ask Mum and Anna. It wasn't very often that anybody ever said "No" to him or didn't give him an immediate answer.

"I'll mention it, John," I managed to say, "I'll mention it and let you know later."

"Mention it? Mention it, young Fynn? More than mention it. Give it some serious thought. I'm sure that a change of scene will do her good."

I was beginning to feel that he was getting me into a corner and I was unable to get out.

"Think about it, Fynn," he reminded me as I said goodbye. I promised I would as I mounted my bike.

I didn't hurry home that night. I was so surprised at the way things had turned out that I needed time to think, and also a pint of the necessary and a breathing space and time to sort out my thoughts before I got home. The more I thought about it, the more I looked at the possibility that he had

64

arranged the whole thing, right down to Arabella's phone call. But no, that wasn't his way. There was something going on that I didn't know about. I'd simply have to talk to Mum about this puzzling episode when I got back. It was nearly midnight when I finally made it home. Mum was still up waiting for me in the kitchen.

"Well," she asked, "what news?"

"False alarm," I replied. "He looked quite all right to me."

She nodded her head as she said, "A bout of indigestion probably. Can be nasty, that can be."

I was still so undecided about the last few hours that I thought it might be better if I spoke of his offer, or was it a request, after I had slept on it. Anna was sound asleep so I wasn't going to be faced with an unending stream of questions this night. By the light of the street lamp, I could see her quite clearly and the only word that came to me at that moment was innocence. After an hour or two, that was the word that ended my waking hours. Whatever else, she was innocence. That was her.

Waking up to my early morning cup of tea brought by Anna, the word "innocence" came into my mind. Innocence. What a nice word that was, even with all its risks. She sat on

the side of my bed and kissed me with all
the fire of a young child. Innocent certainly.
And then it came to me that I had never realized what responsibility that quality placed
on older people. Not that I had any doubt
about John at all. It was simply that I had
no idea why John wanted to see her so much.
Mentally, I added another word to Innocence
and that was "Trust."

Over breakfast we talked about John's request. Mum didn't see that she would come to any harm, and after all it would certainly make a change to get out of all the smoke and dust for a few days.

"You don't suppose he's trying to change her mind about going to church, do you?" Mum asked me.

That was something I had never really thought about, but I was absolutely certain that he would never do a thing like that. As for Anna, the thought of seeing all the rabbits, birds and the odd deer was very pleasing to her. The fly in the ointment was being away from her friends . . . Bombom, Matt, Millie and the rest of the gang. She gave it a great deal of thought. As I got ready for work, she made up her mind.

"Fynn," she yelled, "if you can come too, it would be very nice. Can you ask Mister John and, say, Fynn, will you?"

I promised that I would get in touch with John before I returned home that evening.

"That's the best plan," said Mum. "I'd feel a lot easier in my mind to know that she wasn't alone with strange people in a strange house, and do try and find out why the Professor wants her to come, will you? I know she's as bright as a bag of buttons, but I don't know what she could possibly say that would be of any use to him."

I promised that I would do my best to get answers to all of these questions and that we would talk about it more when I returned.

Anna walked with me to the top of the street. "Fynn, when I get bigger, you can go to work on your tandem and I can drive it home and then come and get you, like the Posh people do, can't I, Fynn?"

"All in good time," I replied, "don't rush growing up too quickly, Tich."

"I'm going to grow up like you," she said. "Just like you!"

I was certainly very pleased and flattered by her last remark but I couldn't help hoping as I pedalled along to work that she might grow up to be a bit better than I was.

I managed to finish off my work in good time that day and by six o'clock, knocking-off time, I was ready to go.

"What's the rush, Fynn? Wait for me and I'll treat you to a pint of wallop," said Cliff.

"He wants to see his lady love. Who is it tonight, Fynn? Blonde or brunette?" asked Ted.

"Neither," I replied. "As a matter of fact, it is a red-head."

"Oh!" said Cliff, "you mean little Anna. Right, Fynn?"

"Right," I answered.

"Keeps you busy, don't she. She'll wreck your love life if you're not careful. What's she up to this time? What does she want now? A tin of canal water or have you got to pick a bunch of flowers for her?"

"Never seen one like her," said Ted.

"Regular ball of fire, that's her!"

"She certainly is a real corker and that's a fact," replied Ted.

"You're right there," I said. "What I want is forty-eight hours a day. Twenty-four hours just ain't enough."

So I pedalled out to Random Cottage. I rang the bell at the back door. Arabella opened it.

"Fynn," she exclaimed, "you're a mess! Whatever has happened to you?"

It was then that I realized that I was still in my overalls and that I was not a very pretty sight to see.

"Come in, do come in. You'd better take off your shoes, though. Can't have you tramping all that oil onto my carpet. You can sit in the kitchen, but make sure you put that newspaper on the chair first. I'll fetch John for you and then I'll make you some tea. I hope you won't keep him too long. Our supper will be ready soon."

I promised that I would be as quick as possible.

"Hello, young Fynn," John greeted me.

"Whatever is amiss?" And after looking at me for a moment and wrinkling up his nose, he said, "Is this the latest fashion that the young are wearing these days? You look a sight! What can I do for you, Fynn? Money or a new pair of trousers? Perhaps you'd like a bath?"

He was really going at it. He was in one of his sarcastic moods. I took no notice of him. I had heard this kind of thing all too often. I prayed that he would never have this approach with Anna. I did try to give her message to him as gently as I could, but it didn't come out quite right.

"Anna said she ain't coming unless I come too. So does Mum."

He chuckled. "Frightened of the ogre, is that it?"

"No," I replied, "that's not it, but, well, you can be a bit sharp-tongued at times and you know it. Anyhow, what do you want to talk to her about?"

"Trust, trust. Where is your trust, young Fynn? Surely you should know me better than that by now, young Fynn?"

He was beginning to make me ashamed of myself.

"Sorry, John," I managed to say. "It's just that she is so very young and if anybody was ever to hurt her, I'd, well, I'd . . ."

"Break them in two," he suggested. "Don't worry, Fynn. I'd help you!"

"But, John," I continued, "whatever would you want to talk to her about? What you know compared with what she knows; it just doesn't make sense."

"If that's meant to be a compliment, I accept it with pleasure."

"Why, John? Why, then?"

"She's an exceedingly bright young lass and will no doubt reach a very high level, but it isn't that that puzzles me. She has caused me to look again at some of the things that I have missed. Now, now, Fynn. No revelation. No road to Damascus or anything like that."

"What then?"

"Perhaps you've never noticed it, Fynn. It is simply the fact that she has this nice ability to use the right words for the right subject, unlike our local Vicar. I just like listening to her. She is one of the few people who makes me think, as you do sometimes."

I felt a bit better after that remark, that sort didn't come very often from John.

On my way home I was at least satisfied that my dear old Master would be on his very best behaviour and that in no way would he cause Anna any distress. I was also happy to hear from him that he would break anybody in two if she was in any way harmed. It was a certain fact that she was a joy to listen to; that unending prattle and question, but I still had no idea exactly what it was that he expected her to say. Perhaps I might just understand more fully when we went to stay with him. Mum was very relieved when I had finished telling her about John.

"Well," she said, "that's all right then. What do you think about it all then, Luvey?"

"I'm glad Fynn can come with me. I wouldn't go else." Then after a moment's thought, Anna said, "Can't Bombom come too, Fynn? Can't she?"

"Well," I replied, "I don't really see how we could ask him to do that. Perhaps another time, if he asks us again. I could find out and then she might go with you without me."

"Wouldn't go," she said flatly. "Wouldn't go without you."

It's funny how good she could make me feel, and what's more I did know that she meant it, too.

"So," said Mum, "what's the arrangement then? Going on the bike?"

"Not this time," I replied. "We're going by car!"

"A real car, Fynn? A really real one?"

"Yes, Mister John is going to collect us here at ten o'clock next Saturday morning and he will bring us home about eight o'clock on Sunday evening."

"Can I go and tell Bombom, eh, please? Can't Bombom and May come to Mister John's house on Sunday after tea and then he could bring us back all together, can't he?"

"Well, he could, I suppose. We'll have to

ask him when he comes on Saturday. You are quite certain you wouldn't like Hec and Sandy and Doreen, Sally, Sarah and the rest of your friends?"

"Could they all get in the car, Fynn? Could they? Fynn, you're teasing me ain't you?"

I nodded. "Off you go to Bombom then and mind you're back in ten minutes."

She fled down the passage. It was always easy in our house to tell when Anna was coming in or going out. Her speed always made the gas light flicker.

"I suppose," said Mum, "I'd better start getting some clothes together."

Then "Oh," she said, "what are we going to do about a nightie for her? I haven't got the time. Got any money in the tin?"

"About two pounds I reckon," I replied.

"That'll do fine. I can get a couple for that. Better get her a pair of knickers while I'm about it."

"Can't see her in a nightie myself. You know that she won't sleep in anything but my shirt."

"I know," she replied, "but it is a special occasion and I wouldn't want to embarrass the child."

"Take a lot more than that to embarrass her. She wouldn't turn a hair if she hadn't got a stitch to her back."

"But still," she said, "they are not like us, are they? With that big house and all that fine stuff they've got."

I laughed. "Never thought of you as a snob. Couldn't live there myself. I'd be far too scared to touch anything."

By seven o'clock the next morning our clothes had been washed and ironed. "Can I go in the street, please? I've got to say good-bye to Bombom and May."

"Some people do sleep, you know," I said. "Even if you get up with the birds other people don't. Besides, we're not going away for ever. Off you go then and try not to make yourself dirty."

"I won't," she promised. "Fynn," she yelled, "will you get my bag too, please? I might want something." So I fetched her bag and placed it beside the case.

"Whatever has she got in there?" asked Mum. "All her pencils and chalks I suppose. What would she do without them?"

By a quarter to ten that morning most of the street knew that we were to be away for two days, and had turned out to see the motor car.

"Hi, Fynn!" yelled Millie. "Off to the moon?"

"Looks like it, doesn't it!"

I was just about to light up a fag when the whirlwind struck me amidships once again. "You won't forget to ask Mister John, Fynn, will you? And if he says 'yes' you can telephone Mr Thackeray, can't you?"

At ten promptly John turned his car into the street. "Can I get in the front, Fynn? Do you reckon Mister John will let me honk the horn?"

A few more "Can I's?" plus a couple of "Do you think's?" and we were off. That was, of course, after she had finished her symphony on the horn, and with Anna directing John as to which way he must go, since she certainly wasn't going to let any of her friends miss seeing her in a car. With me spread out comfortably over the large back seat and Anna chattering next to John, we slowly went on our way. John was a very careful driver and he needed to be even more so at this moment, for he had to duck more than once as she flung out an arm to indicate some event or situation that we passed. "Look, Mister John, look at that!"

"What's that, Mister John, what is it?" But he was fully concentrating on ducking out-flung arms and trying to get us there in one piece.

We got there eventually. John was thankful that he had got home intact. He had never experienced that kind of journey before!

Arabella greeted us at the front door. Although we had been there a number of times before, we had always used the back door and she had never shown us the house. We had not seen more than the dining-room and perhaps had a passing peak at the sitting-room.

"Come along in you two. I'll show you to your rooms and then you can explore the house, but," she added, "please don't touch anything. We don't use that room," she explained, pointing to a closed door, "nor that one and that one is mine. You can look at it if you want to."

We were taken upstairs. I had a double bed whilst Anna had a single. I helped her put her clothes away in the drawer.

"How did this get in here?" I asked her as she drew my shirt from her bag.

"That's for the night time, Fynn. That's the shirt you gived me."

"Whatever happened to those two nighties I bought you?"

"Took 'em out!" she exclaimed. "They were too nice for sleeping in. I like this best," she continued, holding up the shirt. Arabella returned just as Anna was holding my shirt. It was a good one.

"Whatever have you got there?" she asked.

"For sleeping in, don't I, Fynn?"

I could do nothing else but nod my head.

"I'll find you an old blouse of mine," responded Arabella. "You can't go to sleep in a thing like that!"

Anna could. She liked it.

A few minutes later, Arabella returned with one of her blouses, all lace and frills in pink and white. "You can have that," Anna was told.

We didn't really have all that much to unpack, so we set off to explore the house. Everything was a bit of a mystery to Anna. She just did not understand why you went to bed in all that frilly stuff. "I mean, what's the point if nobody is going to see it?"

And as for all those rooms that apparently were never used, well, I ask you, you just had to be a bit doolally to do a thing like that!

As for real hot water coming out of a tap! Just fancy not having to boil a kettle of water or light up the copper!

"They must be real millionaires, Fynn, mustn't they?"

"They are what people call 'very comfortably off'," I explained.

I suppose her biggest surprise was that she was unable to find the bath hanging on the wall, in the back yard or anywhere.

"Don't they have a bath then, Fynn?"

So off we went upstairs again in order to see the bathroom. She tried as hard as she could to move it. "It's stuck, Fynn. Help me."

It was difficult for her to accept the fact that I wouldn't be able to move it either, for it was fixed. It took her a long time before she would believe that one!

For the next thirty minutes we just mooched about the house, looking at everything and in all the rooms that were not locked up. We saw the new-fangled carpet cleaner, the electric boiler, the solid fuel cooker and such like things. Anna walked with her hands held behind her back.

"What's up, Tich? Got a pain?"

"She told me not to touch anything, so I'm not."

"I think she meant don't mess about with things."

"I'm not going to," she replied. Knowing her so well after these few years, I figured that there was a thing or two not to her liking. As we walked in the garden I said, "Don't you like it, Sweetie? Wouldn't you like to live here?"

"Nope," she snapped at me. "I like it home with Mum better! I suppose some people might like to live here, but not me." She continued to tell me why, before I had a chance to ask her.

"Fynn, it's all too sort of special and all those things that you have to look after that's supposed to look after you, well, well you just never get no time to play and enjoy yourself."

I had never heard labour-saving devices spoken of like that before, but I suppose it might be true sometimes. She wasn't at all keen either that there weren't any trains passing the window, nor was there any street light coming in.

"I'm going to sleep in your room tonight, Fynn. That's what I'm going to do and then we can talk."

I wasn't sure how Arabella would take all these criticisms about her house and only hoped she wouldn't ask any awkward question.

Anna was surprised to find that John had another way of doing sums. He had told her mathematics was "like playing a game." That was new to her. She didn't understand. He explained the difference. "When you play a game in the street, my little maid, you can't unkick a ball and you can't unthrow a stone. Once you've done a thing, there is no going back. But with sums and mathematics, there is always a way that you can go back."

That afternoon he showed her two moving films he had made many years previously. I had never seen them. I didn't even know that his main hobby was making films. One was based on a game of draughts and the other was a game of chess. No people and no hands appeared in the film; just the pieces doing what they were supposed to do. It really did look like a game. Because he could vary the speed of the projector. He could make it look like anything from a pointless, dizzy muddle to a proper game. Anna liked it. It was just like being two different people, one seeing things fast and the other seeing things slow. It was no wonder I got in such a muddle with all these different Annas knocking about. The one that saw things slowly, the one that saw things speeded up, to say nothing of the one on this side of the road and the one on the other. Her different perspectives were such that sometimes she reminded me of the story of Dick Turpin, who was seen to come out of the Black Swan Inn at York and ride off in several directions at the same time!

"Ain't God wonderful?"

Along with so many people in the 1930s, John was convinced that, given a few more years, Science would be able to explain everything that was worthy of explanation. He had little time or inclination to believe anything that wasn't capable of proof, or at least some sort of reasonable explanation. He held to this belief so firmly that on any possible occasion, he would launch into a lengthy talk on the subject, along with a total dismissal of the significance of the more gentle things of life around him. As I have mentioned, both his house and his garden were so well organized, with a place for everything and everything in its proper place, that anything slightly out of order was such a blight on the total organization that it had to be put right instantly. Anna viewed this order with suspicion and sadness.

"It's like bloody wallpaper. It's the same thing what just goes on and on! Don't it?"

As she was looking at the garden, John came up behind us.

"Do you like it, little one?"

"No!" She was never one to dodge the awkward things.

"Don't you like flowers, Mister John?" We were looking at blocks of red flowers, blocks of yellow flowers and that kind of thing.

John was more than a little perplexed. "Can't you see that I do? I've spent a lot of time and money on this garden!"

"But not lo . . . !"

I knew she was going to say "love them" but changed her mind and asked Mister John, "Why don't you let them do what they want?"

"Why in heaven's name should a flower want to do anything? It hasn't the ability to *want* anything!"

Anna could contain her displeasure longer than most, but in the end she broke out with that scornful word: "Pooh!" She turned away from the flowers and headed for what, according to John, was the untidiest part of the garden, the part that was going to be tidied up next spring and turned into a real garden. John and I followed after her.

"Don't you like my garden, my little maid?"

She shook her head vigorously. She had no need to think of her answer. That had been ready for a long time. "Mister John, it looks like a war," was her unflattering comment.

Poor John was completely taken aback. "War?"

She nodded. "All them flowers look like soldiers on parade," she said and marched like a toy soldier around the border. John managed to restrain himself except for a little "Oh!"

As we went in for tea, I hoped Arabella

wasn't going to ask if she liked the house. I knew that there were a few more "Noe's" lurking around somewhere. But she did ask. It wasn't a "No" this time. She looked around the room and said, "It looks like that enchanted castle. You know, Fynn, like the one in the book you gived me."

I didn't remember the castle and I didn't like the way she dragged me into the discussion. It was a sure sign that something was going to happen. I got that itchy feeling again, but Arabella and John didn't understand the sign and they glowed to hear that they lived in an enchanted castle. They weren't quite ready for, "You know, Fynn, that one where the people went to sleep for a hundred years."

I wished that I was asleep too! She'd started it, so she could finish it, but no, she had got me into it and all I could do was to sit it out and hope that their looks would soon soften!

I never have been able to work out why it is that you spend years teaching children to be honest and truthful and then along come those times when you hope that they have forgotten that teaching! It happened to me often. I'd hope that she wasn't going to be too honest or too truthful, but she always was. *She* didn't mind one bit, but it often left me floundering. I suppose it's just one of those things you have to put up with. The order in John's garden and house was similar to the order in his mind. There was nothing random in all of this except for the name. For Arabella and John spring-cleaning lasted all year and every year. I must say I did enjoy the sharp edges of John's mind, especially when he launched into some complicated explanation, like the beauty of some involved geometric diagram or the shape of a mathematical formula. This was always a pleasure to me, but it wasn't always so for Anna. The "Skeletons" as she called these diagrams and formulae were all very well, but she was after the meat. She wanted to put clothes on the "Skeletons" and that was what she was about.

We had listened to him for most of the afternoon on one of our visits. I wasn't doing all that well with his explanations. The idea that sooner or later the whole thing, atoms, stars and even Anna was going to be described by a few physical laws in a mathematical form, was a struggle for me. I had looked at Anna frequently, but she showed no sign of distress. I thought that by now we should have had an explosion or two, but they never came.

"Mister John," she asked, "will you know everything about Fynn and me too?"

"Oh," he said, with some surprise, "I'd forgotten you were there."

This news was strange to her and it took her a couple of fizzy drinks and the odd cake or two before she managed to stow away the important bits of John's talk. She was always the master of the "poor little me act." It always left me feeling helpless, but I knew it was a danger sign.

"Mister John," she said, "I'm such a little bit of it all, ain't I?"

"Yes, my dear, as I am, and Fynn."

"Here it comes," I said to myself, "I hope you're ready, John."

"Mister John," she said all too sweetly.

"Yes, my dear, what is it?"

"Why does such a little bit like me want to understand it all? It's such a big bit, ain't it?"

John tried to find the right words to answer her, but they just wouldn't come out. Anna wasn't at all frightened of bloody Skeletons and she certainly wasn't going to give up.

"What about them flowers then, they're littler than me? What about if the flowers want to understand too, what about it? That's why they want to play and you won't let them."

It was more than a question, more like an accusation, and poor John didn't know what to do with it. It was quite clear to me the way he shook his head that John did not like that question at all. For him it wasn't a real question. It sounded all right to me and I wanted to know the answer. If it was all going to end up in a handful of laws, then it would be nice to know why a little bit of the universe should want to know and understand the rest of it. Perhaps I had simply missed a step or two on the way. It seemed to me that John had discarded Mister God so completely that I never did grasp the difference between a universe that understood itself and the Mister God that Anna talked about. It seemed to me, at times, that they were like a couple of bridge builders, trying to build a bridge across a chasm, and they had left me stuck in the middle, just hanging on with nowhere to put my feet down. It was strange to be sandwiched between this pair, old John so full of knowledge and logic but so short of imagination, and that little red-headed imp, full of invention and imagination, but a little short on fact. But I really did want to know why the little bit wants to understand the big bit. Why should a daisy want to understand a star? So far as I could figure it out, the only thing that wanted to understand was the bit in the middle somewhere, the soul or the mind. There never was such an ill-matched pair as these two, but in some curious way they were able to spark each other off. Not that I'm complaining too much, mind you, but all this stuff was at times too much for me. I wasn't doing too badly with John's set of rules and his way of going about things, and I think I could just about manage Anna's set of rules, the red hot way, but it did mean that I was in danger of either being frozen to death by John or burnt alive by Anna!

There were many times when I reckoned that Anna must have had a little knob tucked away somewhere — one that I never found.

If she had such a knob, I knew that the instruction would be "Simmer gently until done and bring to a fast rolling boil." But, as I didn't know where she kept it and neither did anybody else, there was always a danger of setting it at the wrong position, as I knew to my cost. For the last week or so it had been set to the simmer position. There was something on her mind. We were going off to have tea with John that afternoon, and, as we had plenty of time to spare, I took a more leisurely route on the tandem, just looking at things. John greeted us at the door. "Ah! The little brat herself and young Fynn."

"Sir," she said.

I had finished that kind of thing some time ago. So, "Hello John."

On the table beside his chair was an open atlas. "Bringing back old memories," he said. "I spent some time there." He prodded his finger in the general direction of France.

"Where's 'there,' Mister John?"

He turned a few pages and prodded again.

"Can't see your house Mister John, can we?"

"Not on this map. I'll show you on another map." He fetched a large scale ordinance map. "There we are, just there. Just where that road is."

Though she had got her own atlas, she had

never seen one on a different scale before, and for the next hour or so John was kept busy with telling her about maps; that one of a scale of this many inches to the mile was either better, or maybe worse, than one of that many miles to the inch.

"Look, Fynn, look at this. Did you know that?"

"Yes," I replied.

"You didn't tell me, did you?"

"You didn't ask."

It was at about this point that the knob was

turned to the "fast rolling boil" stage.

"Mister John," she so exploded it was almost possible to see the steam coming out of her ears, "Mister John, if you could make a map squillions of miles to the inch and then one squillions of inches to the mile, you could see them things, couldn't you?"

"What things are they, my little one?"

"Them electron things wot Fynn reads about. Then you would know if you could divide them, couldn't you?"

John looked at me. All I could do was to shrug my shoulders. She hadn't quite finished yet. "You could put it in yer ear, couldn't you?"

I never did find out why very small things always had to get put in your ear. Never mind. I suppose if you really could draw a map of the whole universe on that kind of scale you might easily put it in your ear.

John really should have left it there and got on with his beer. At this rate he might never finish it, but no, he just would go on telling her all about number scales, like in ordinary counting, where successive places were units, tens, hundreds, thousands, tens of thousands and so on, and the other ways where the successive places were units, threes, nines, twenty-seven and so on and so forth, to say nothing of all the other ways of doing it. It was the idea of reduction and enlargement that captured Anna's imagination, despite John's insistence that it was not possible to do that kind of thing because there are physical limits to what the mind can grasp. All he got was, "In your head you can, can't you?"

There was really no answer to that one. I was pleased that it had been his turn and not mine to be the target of her ideas. I thought it was going to stay that way, but that was too much to hope for.

"Fynn," she exclaimed, "you can do sums with the angels, can't you?"

"I suppose you must be able to," I agreed, "but I don't know how."

"You can find out, then, can't you? and then you can tell me, can't you?"

The problem with memories is not that they aren't true. It's just that there's so much of them to write down. All those things that have happened to me over the last umpteen years would take about ten or so times longer to write down than they took to happen. But then you don't have to put down the unpleasant bits, merely the nice bits; those little gems or words that were said all those years ago that meant so much to me then. I just don't know if they are as true as they seemed to me to be at the time. Old John's often-quoted saying that "True mathematics is a lost art of civilization" or that "Mathematics is nothing more than unconscious art." Or Mum's remark that "The brain is the organ of learning and the mind is the garden of knowledge." These kinds of sayings still look fresh to me, even though my own garden of knowledge is always in danger of being taken over by the usual crop of weeds, and I find it takes me a long time to get rid of them. But I've never found a better way of saying things so I guess I'll stick with them.

And then there was that lovely but strange thing that Anna had said, and that I never quite understood. After a couple of years of pretty concentrated mathematical studies, she suddenly floored me one night with her usual mixture of maths and religion.

"Fynn," she began, "it's a funny thing, ain't it?"

"Must be," I replied, "but what is?"

"Religion." She had thumped me on my head.

"How funny?" I asked.

A few more thumps. "It reduces you in size and increases you in dimensions."

"Hey, Tich, where did you get that from?"

"Saw it in one of your books."

I was amazed that she had cottoned onto

that, for it is the kind of thing that even if you don't understand you don't want to forget or throw away. It sounds so good that it might even be true; that is, if I can ever figure out what it truly means. Maybe one day I will, but in the meantime I'll keep it safe! There are so many words inside me. Things that either Mum or Anna or John have said. Things that really sound so good that I don't like to get rid of them, even though I don't understand them. But I will one day.

My life was now full of puzzles and riddles, like the occasion when John was trying to tell me the difference between applied and pure mathematics.

"Just remember, young Fynn," he said, "applied mathematics is when you search for the solution to the problem, but pure mathematics, ah! that is when you search for the problem of the solution."

It was odd that he could so often say that kind of thing, but found it so difficult to understand Mum when she had told him that Anna wasn't looking for a needle in a haystack, but rather looking for the haystack in the needle. Even if she did change the word "haystack" to "God," I think I did understand. And, of course, Millie could also come out with the odd "doughnut saying" that could so easily stand me on my head. But then I had known Millie for about ten years. She had a heart of gold and a wit to match. We had been talking about love. In view of the way that Millie made her money as a prostitute that might seem a bit odd to some people. I said that I found it very difficult to understand just what love was.

"You had better ask Anna," she had said. "I think it's got something to do with seeing in others the mystery of yourself."

It was very early in 1935. At sixteen, I was among the oldest of John's students. In those days, most boys left school at fourteen years of age. For many it was a time to rejoice, to get away from school at long last. For others it was a matter of necessity to earn some money to help out the family. For them the lack of money was a perpetual worry. I was one of the lucky ones, with a small bursary and various odd jobs. Mum had persuaded me to stay on. She had a job, too. Although we had no money to waste we were a lot better off than most people. I was happy to continue my education, as by now John had asked me to demonstrate experiments in chemistry and physics against the background of his lectures. On this day he hadn't told me to prepare anything. He lurched in in his usual way.

"Today," he said, "I have good news for you. In a few months' time I retire."

There was the odd subdued cheer from some boys, but for most of us it didn't seem possible.

"As from that happy date, Mr Clement will shoulder the impossible task of knocking sense into your heads, not that it will do any good. Some of you blockheads are so thick that I very much doubt if anything could penetrate those dark recesses of your minds."

He was in his sarcastic mood again and he flowed on for ten minutes or so. "Ah well," he ended, "it will no longer be my responsibility. In the meantime, we have much to do and do it you will."

My world had suddenly shifted its orbit. I wasn't at all happy about this unexpected news, but at the moment I didn't know how John's retirement was going to affect me. It didn't seem possible that I wasn't going to see him every day. As my father had died so early on in my life it was John that I had taken my puzzles and problems to, and without him . . . I guess I loved that old grouch, but I wasn't going to tell him.

We were to assemble in the big hall to bid him farewell and to see the usual presentation. I couldn't face that. It was too much. I didn't turn up. I wasn't going to cry, not in front of everybody. If I wanted to bloody well cry I'd do it alone. I had a very special place I went to on important occasions — one of the little bridges over the canal. Nobody used it very often. It was tucked away down a back street, with a nice view over the park. I had sat straddled across the parapet for hours doing nothing much. I couldn't think what came next. I knew that somebody had called my name but hell, so what?

"Fynn, Fynn, where the devil are you? Don't be a bloody fool. Speak up, Boy! Speak up! I haven't got all day to waste for an answer!"

The same old impatient Master walked over the bridge and stood beside me. "What, no goodbyes, young Fynn? Aren't I worth a good-bye?"

"Bugger off!" I spat at him. "Just bugger off." I didn't mean to say that and I regretted my words immediately. I wanted to say something else but I couldn't. "Who told you I was here? Why can't you leave me alone?"

"I asked your mother. She told me. It's a nice place to come to when you want to think, isn't it? As for your words, I do understand. I really do. Even at my ripe old age. I understand. My car is only just down the road. Let's go for a little jaunt, shall we, and we can have a long talk."

Seated in the car he had taken my hand in his. He had never done that before. The only times he touched me had been with that three-foot length of bunsen burner tubing when he punished me, which was often.

"What's bothering you, Fynn? What's on your mind?"

With my hand in his I still couldn't say the words I wanted to. All I managed to say were the words of a child, a lost child.

"I won't see you again, will I?"

"Oh that," he said, "don't worry about that. I don't intend that to happen." We drove slowly through the park and headed off across the marshes.

"What's your plan?"

"Suppose I'll have to get a job."

"Don't be too hasty. There's plenty of time. Finish off your education and then wait until after the term ends. Mister Clement won't bully you like I have done and he really does know his subject. And as for not seeing me — you know where I live, you know my telephone number and it's hardly any distance at all to Random Cottage, and you can come to see me at any time at all. In fact, not only may you come, I ask you to come. You can still pursue your studies with me. You have the promise of good things and well . . . just come whenever you like. Is that what you want?"

That was what I wanted. It felt like old times again.

"I've packed my persuader," he chuckled. "I couldn't be without that."

So it was that, although I didn't see John so often, I did see him for more hours in the week than I had previously done.

It was quite true what John had said. Mr Clement really was a nice person and certainly he knew his subject. I suppose it was because the persuader was no longer there that it happened that after a number of elaborate practical jokes and one thing and another, I was politely asked to leave the school. Had Old John still been there with his trusty persuader, I would have had to do my studies standing up. But it wasn't like that any longer. Things had changed a bit. With John, punishment was over and done with quickly, but being reported was quite another matter. We all missed the persuader and it really didn't hurt all that much. John had never said "this hurts me more than it hurts you." He knew better, and so far as he was concerned it was supposed to hurt and he was no weakling, especially not with the old persuader in his hand. I had complained on one occasion when it caught me in the wrong place and he didn't apologize. Not him.

"Last week," he said, "after that rugger match, you were not a very pretty sight with a missing front tooth, a beautiful black eye and a nose bleed. And you enjoyed yourself! I'm merely trying to give you more pleasure — something more you can brag about."

Suddenly I was out to work, meeting other people and making other friends. And then there was Anna as well.

After a very few meetings with Anna, John was convinced of one thing, as he told me one evening when I had gone over to see him.

"This untutored and uncontrolled talent of Anna's really must be helped to develop in an orderly fashion."

"Sure," I replied. "How do you go about doing that?"

"She needs proper teaching," he said. "I know you've done your best to help her, young Fynn, but you will surely agree that you haven't been trained to teach her, have you?"

I had to admit that the only training that I had had was as one of his pupils.

"I know that I taught you, but that was how to learn, not how to teach."

I wanted to give John a good answer to that, but the words would not come. So far as I could make out, Anna and I managed to teach each other. We were both Students *and* Teachers, and the most important thing for me was to be the Student and her the Teacher. I didn't tell him that. It wasn't the kind of thing to say to a man with all that experience and knowledge, so I didn't bother to say anything.

"Although I am now retired, I am very willing to help her with her studies."

"You'll have to talk to Mum first and see what she says," I told him. "And you'll have to talk to Anna, too."

"No, Fynn, I will certainly talk to your

mother, but you will have to persuade the child."

I agreed to talk to Anna, but I wasn't going to press her into it. To tell the truth, I wasn't at all keen on this idea of John's but I would never stand in her way, if that was what she really wanted. I just wanted to do whatever was best for Anna.

It took us a few days to sort it all out. Mum finally agreed that it was worth a try for a little while, to see how it went. It was more difficult to talk to Anna about it. Her first response was "No."

"Don't you want to learn?" I asked her.

"Course I do."

"Then why the 'No'?"

The way she explained it all to me made it sound simple, and I reckon Mister God saw the sense in it too, but I had a feeling that John wouldn't. His insistence that everything had to be neat and tidy was matched by Anna's insistence that it shouldn't. They were poles apart.

Unlike John, I had given up any attempt to understand the way Anna's mind worked some time ago. I was content just to let things happen, and rescue her, if I could, from whatever muddle she might get herself into. When I couldn't, Mum was the one who understood her most. She knew that she might be hurt at times, but that's the way it had to be. "There was really no safe way to grow up" as Mum put it in her upside down way. "There might be a safer way than this to grow older, but there just ain't no safe way to grow up." Both Mum and Anna did this kind of thing to me. They would so often answer my simple question, or puzzle, by a harder one and I complained. "I'm surprised you haven't worked that one out yet," she would say. She never did have much schooling, but she had packed a lot of experience into her life. How often she had laid her finger on my lips and said, "No questions, wait. That is too difficult to do when you are young. That's what happens when you grow up. That's what life is for." Poor Mum, she didn't understand, did she?

She very rarely got angry but she did one day in her own quiet way. "You and your precious Master! The pair of you make me sick!! You *see* everything and *understand* nothing important!!!"

"Come on, Mum; easy. What does Anna do that I don't?"

She had softened my pain by cupping my face in her hands. She had smiled when she said, "You never notice what you see most often. Neither does Mister John. Anna does."
She waited for a moment or two before she

went on "That's what's called 'discovery'."

Having delivered herself of this little gem, she took a sheet of paper and wrote two words "Look" and "See."

"There," she said, "the word 'look' has got two eyes open and the word 'see' has got two eyes half shut."

I thought I could see what she was on about, but this wasn't the way that John had taught me. "That's not scientific, Mum, that's just fancy."

"They didn't teach you much, did they? Science is all right, but it's not everything."

I wasn't going to argue with her, but I didn't agree with her.

"What is science," she said, "but the discovery of the rules behind the facts? It never occurs to your precious Mister John that there is something else."

"What else can there be?" I asked.

"There's always the facts behind the rules and that's religion, that is."

I nearly said they were just different sides of the same coin, but decided against it. I was almost certain to get myself into an even greater muddle. This was the problem when talking to experts in "doughnut speech."

When I got home it was all over. Arthur had arrived safe and sound, Nurse Turner was satisfied and most of the people who had waited around outside Mrs Jones's front door had left. The only person in the street who had only a vague idea of all the excitement and drama was me, and I was soon to learn.

"Fynn, have you ever seen a baby come out?"

"Out? Out of what?"

"Fynn, don't be silly. You know, born."

"No, babies I never have. Kittens I have. Puppies I have. But babies never. Why?"

"Do you know what they do?"

"No, what?"

"They turn it upside down and smack its bum. That's what they do."

"What would they want to do a thing like that for?" I asked.

"Don't know. The nurse didn't tell me. I wonder why they turn it upside down?"

This turning of a thing upside down was something Anna understood very well. It made you see things properly, so perhaps turning a baby upside down wasn't a bad way for it to start off its life. But smacking its bum she wasn't sure of. It was all real doughnut stuff. I wondered if John was ready for this kind of stuff. He surely must know about it. What would he do when it happened to him? I reckoned it was going to. John did seem to be very confident that teaching Anna was

going to be a fairly straightforward thing to do. He was in for a surprise, I guess.

The first week went quite well. There were, of course, the odd hold ups but nothing much except the full blast of her puzzles on our way home.

On those journeys I always took the safe route because the way Anna wriggled about on my handlebars made the canal route tricky.

"Fynn, Mister John took my picture today and, Fynn, I really and truly was upside down. Everything is."

John's large plate camera definitely showed things to be upside down. Either that, or she was. And, at that time, she didn't know which. What with being upside down sometimes and back to front in a looking glass, it was going to take quite a bit of working out and if John wasn't very careful, he was going to find himself turned inside out too!

"Know why it's upside down and inside out, Fynn? You know why?"

"Tell me when we get home, not now, or you'll have us both base over apex in the middle of the road."

Little things like that were of lesser importance to her than telling me why everything, everything was upside down. " 'Cos," she yelled, "Mister God ain't finished us yet."

"If you don't sit still," I told her, "he's never going to get a chance."

"Fynn, when we get finished properly, then we will all be the right way up." I was glad to know that. It was a real comfort to me!

Over our supper we were treated to her nonstop chatter on the finer points of dividing one fraction by another. All you had to do was to turn one of them upside down, or was it both of them? She couldn't quite remember and perhaps it didn't matter. It came as no surprise to her, this business of turning things upside down in order to understand them. She was an expert in that kind of thing, and so was Mum with her "doughnut speech." I was a little envious of John in his teaching of Anna, but I was comforted by her saying, "He ain't half as good as you, Fynn, he gets a bit muddled." I wasn't going to tell him that. He'd never believe me. If she wanted to tell him that he got a bit muddled she would have to do it herself.

The first week of his teaching had gone off fairly well, except, that is, the small matter of living upside down. He had had no experience of that. The second week didn't go at all well. In fact, it was a near-disaster for me. Anna had been showing him some of the interesting things I had shown her months ago. Things with numbers and a chess board. I had used her own words to explain to her, not the kind of words you would find in a text book. For John, the right word was very important, so when she called it "the thingy that Fynn showed me," he almost exploded. I know I should have called it the binomial theorem, but I didn't. It didn't seem important to me then, but it did mean that I got the rough end of his tongue.

"Why in heaven's name did you teach her that, young Fynn? She's nowhere ready for that . . ."

"I didn't," I said, "it just happened. What's the trouble, John, did she get it wrong?"

"No," he replied, "as a matter of fact she explained most of it quite beautifully in her own words, but you really must help her to use the correct words otherwise she will never be understood."

I didn't bother to tell John about the time I had spent explaining to Anna how to use the word terminology: giving names to things and ideas in various subjects. It didn't take her a moment to jump from numbers to Mister God. All those various names he got called, like Allah, the Absolute, Jehovah weren't really all that important, were they? *She*'d stick to Mister God and words like "thingy." Most of her friends had at least three names, some even had four, so it didn't matter what name they were called, they would know that you were talking to them. If it didn't matter to her if she was called Anna or Tich or even "the brat," it certainly wasn't going to matter to Mister God one little bit, was it? It was a lot of fuss about nothing. John was a little put out to be told that he only changed the names, whilst Fynn changed the numbers. She had tried to explain to him that every square on the chess board had its own name, which could be changed, and that depended on what you did. All that the numbers did was to tell you in how many different ways you could get there. It didn't really matter what you called it as long as you got there, did it?

Neither did he like it when I said that all I could give her was a sort of life-raft, even though it did have plenty of holes in it.

"What other bit of nonsense have you managed to teach her? What must I beware of?"

I did tell him that the thing she really wanted to know was how to do sums with the angels and perhaps even Mister God too, and since nobody knew just how many fingers an angel might count on she did understand how the various number bases worked, powers and indices and such like.

"Oh, does she indeed! I will have to see about that. No doubt she is very muddled about that. I really do wish that you had left that to me."

He was soon to find out that doing sums was one thing which wasn't too difficult once you had got the knack. It was her questions afterwards that caused all the trouble. I tried to tell him about those fifty bald-headed men she had asked me about. There was this church and every Sunday fifty bald-headed men came in, each man had a number painted on his head, the numbers from 1 to 50. Up in the dome of the church was an angel with a camera, and every Sunday he took a picture of the numbers painted on their heads, and every Sunday they had to sit in a different order, which was all very well except that she wanted to know, if the vicar was thirty years old, how old would he be when these bald-headed men finally repeated the first pattern. I did work it out for her. As far as I could figure it out, this vicar must have been 5.848864^{62}. So I reckoned that by the time the pattern was repeated he would be far too old to be much concerned with it!! He was going to be a very old man, older than Methuselah, older than good old Tyrannosaurus Rex. Why, if you added the ages of every living person, he'd be a lot older that that! Perhaps he might even be older than . . . No! That's not possible. I knew her answer to that kind of answer.

"Ooh, Fynn, ain't sums wonderful!"

"Yeah, ain't they."

Particularly if somebody else did all the hard work for her. It was good for me when she began to take over the hard work for herself.

From the Rev. Castle's point of view, numbers were totally unimportant and, as for John, since he didn't believe there was a God anyway, going to church was, for him, a complete waste of time. As for the bald-headed men and her other problems, it was simply a matter of combinations and permutations, which was all right for some, but they weren't Anna's words. It all left me struggling in the middle somewhere. What neither of them seemed to understand was something very simple. At least, it was simple the way she put it.

It was a different matter when she asked me to work it out in numbers. That took a long time. She knew quite well that if you did things with little numbers they had the habit of suddenly becoming very, very big numbers, and very, very big numbers were obviously Mister God numbers. For her they both seemed to be the same thing.

The six days of creation looked a bit different after she had finished with them. Not that anybody else was impressed by her ideas. You needed to be with her whilst she explained them to really understand what she was on about. I didn't know that Mister God only made three things on that first day. Although she had no idea what they were and even if there were more than three, it didn't really matter.

"Then he went to sleep," she told me, "and dreamed how he could arrange these three things in different ways. So the next day, when he arranged these three things, he ended up with six things and after that, of course, he had another little sleep and dreamed of all the ways he could arrange six things in their different orders."

And she wasn't at all surprised to find that the answer was 720. She gave up there on the answer to her question: "How many ways can you arrange 720 things — in every possible way?" This was a bit too much for her and it was for me too! What Mister God was going to do on the fifth and sixth days was something only he could do. The number was going to be so big that nobody could ever possibly work it out. It was no wonder he was tired with all them numbers and had a rest on the seventh day!

Though, for Anna, Mister God and very big numbers were the same thing, neither frightened her. They were both lovely and both very beautiful, so they had to be the same, didn't they? Whenever Anna really got into top gear, there was nothing to do but listen until she had finished or dried up. When she was in full flood the only place for her to be was sitting on my lap.

It was a bit of a surprise to John to find her suddenly on his lap. I know that he was pleased with that, but as a Teacher it wasn't the kind of thing that had happened to him before. A couple of hours of this was quite enough for anybody and John was no longer young.

"You'd better take her home now, Fynn, and bring her back tomorrow. I need time to recover. Although for much of the time I didn't know what she was talking about, I must confess I did like listening to her. It is, I suppose, just possible that her chatter makes sense and I wanted to hear more of it, but not now. So take her home and bring her back tomorrow."

Mister John, as Anna called him, was playing an increasing role in the life of us all, so that the day when we took Mum along with us to see him could no longer be put off. So there we all were one afternoon, drinking tea in his sitting room, Anna between Mum and me on the sofa, and John on the other side of the room in his favourite armchair. It was an extraordinary gathering, with three people who were not afraid to say what they thought and who might, at any moment, say it. Of course there was me too, but since I was always being taught by one or other of them, I didn't really count. I was along to see fair play. Although I was fairly certain that this little get-together wasn't going to end up as a free-for-all or a battle royal, I was sure that somebody or other was going to make a mistake sooner or later. Mum was firmly convinced that most people just went on talking when there was nothing else to be said. She did manage to ask John if all this extra teaching was absolutely necessary.

"You wouldn't want her to grow up like a savage in the jungle, would you?"

Anna nodded her head and held my hand.

"I'm not sure of that," replied Mum, "not sure at all."

"Oh, come, come, whatever makes you say that?"

"Well, I've never had your education, but it does seem to me that these so-called savages don't do so bad after all."

"In what way is that?"

"They, at least, do manage to live with their devils and demons and survive, but we live with our successes and fail so often."

What the answer to that one was, I never did know. Neither did John. His next shot also went a bit astray: "Every day she is getting older and every day lost is a day lost for ever." That was a very bad mistake for him to make. Nobody else in the room believed that one. That was pushing education far too hard.

"Lost days indeed," Mum said, "surely there is nothing worth having in this world that is not worth waiting for."

Mum's calm and slow manner put John off completely. She just never seemed to be where he expected her to be.

For the next thirty minutes John and Mum tried to work out some scheme to further Anna's education.

"So," said John finally, "what are we going to do with this extraordinary little Miss?"

The "extraordinary little Miss" giggled and pinched me.

"Why not ask her?" I suggested.

"Not yet," he said. "Are you an extraordinary little Miss?" he asked her.

"Am I, Fynn?"

"Don't know about that!" I laughed. "You're a perishing nuisance sometimes and if *that* is extraordinary, then I guess you are!"

John frowned at my remark and showed his disapproval.

Eventually it was decided that I was to bring Anna to his house and whilst he was helping her with her various lessons, I was to help in his large garden, doing odd jobs about the place. So, instead of bagging up sawdust and that kind of job that occupied my spare time, he was to pay me more than my odd jobs did. That was fine with me.

John wasn't the only one to express strong views on how Anna should be taught. Any more of it and I would begin to think I had let her down. It seemed everybody who came in touch with her seemed to know exactly how it should be done. After a few months of this arrangement, John said to me over a glass of beer, "You know, Fynn, there is only one way to teach Anna properly, at least to teach her in the normal way."

"And what's that, John?" I asked.

"I'm afraid that you'll just have to find the largest possible box there is and keep her away from other people. It's something that nobody in his right mind would do, but I can see no other way. The habit of asking every Tom, Dick and Harry to write things down for her means that her little head is open to every opinion under the sun and every crackpot idea imaginable. She really need only have one good teacher and not these hundreds of poor ones. If only I was twenty years younger, I'd like to take her on regularly, not just for an occasional lesson."

"John," I reminded him, "in case you have forgotten, you did teach me for nearly five years."

"True, very true," he sighed.

"So I can't be all that bad."

"No," he agreed, "as long as you stick to one thing at a time you are not too bad."

"John, do you remember the nickname you had?"

"Which one was that? I've had so many in my time."

"The Black Knight," I replied.

"Oh, that one," he said. "I could never understand why."

"Oh come on, John. Surely you know why."

"No, I don't."

"The way that you would jump from one subject to another could be so very troublesome."

"Oh that! But I did know what I was doing!"

"That's exactly what Anna does too and, as far as I can see, she knows what she's doing too. So maybe I've got a White Knight to teach me now?"

"Perhaps you're right, perhaps you're right, and I suppose," he continued in his sarcastic way, his refuge whenever he was lost for words, "I suppose you consider yourself to be the King."

"Not me," I grinned, "not me. I'm just a pawn. My problem is just that I have to change colour so often."

"Your usual clever stuff, young Fynn!"

"Got it from a clever teacher."

"The thing I find so very puzzling about her," he continued, "is the fact that she will not loosen her grasp on anything, even rubbish, until she understands it, to her own satisfaction that is. If there is anything in this world that might make one say I believe in the human soul, it's the sheer persistence of the child that baffles me. I really don't think she would bat an eyelid if faced by the devil itself. Now look what you've done to me! I am becoming maudlin and sentimental and it won't do, Fynn, it just won't do. Do you know what she asked me last week? She asked me what I would pray for if there was a God and, heaven help me, I told her. You'll laugh at me, Fynn. I told her that in that case I would pray that my butterfly and moth collection could be brought back to life. It's the one thing I feel guilty about. There, you see, between the pair of you I'm getting a bit soft in the head, and I don't like it."

Then came the day she ran into the garden calling my name. I did manage to catch her in my arms before she fell into a flower bed.

"Fynn, Fynn. Come quick. Mister John fell over and he can't get up."

He didn't look all that bad when we entered the sitting-room, a little pale perhaps, nothing that a tankard of ale wouldn't put right. But the Doctor, when he came, had other ideas. He was old, he was tired, he mustn't get excited and suddenly Anna's extra teaching came to an end.

"Will you please continue to tend the garden and do little jobs for me?" he asked.

"Of course I will."

"Please bring the little maid with you whenever you come and a few friends too, if that is what she wants. They can play in the garden and Anna can talk to me and we can all have tea together later."

Although Anna seemed to have a fairly firm grip on many ideas, she wasn't all that good when it came to adding up numbers. It isn't my strongest point either, for that matter. Perhaps it was my love of mathematics that made her feel that it was this subject that was very important to understand. The problem was that at school, it was just one tedious round of doing sums like adding, taking away and multiplying. Things like that. So far as she could see, all that kind of stuff didn't matter a hoot.

What she really wanted to do was to know how she could talk to angels, Mister God and, who knows, perhaps even people who lived out there in the stars. The difficulty was she just didn't know how this could be done.

"Fynn," she said, "how can you do sums with angels?"

I was slightly taken off balance by this question. I didn't quite see why angels would want to do sums. Anyway, I reckoned they didn't have time for that sort of thing. So I answered her with, "Why would they want to do sums anyway?"

"Don't know," she replied, "but they might."

"Suppose so," I managed to say, "but I honestly don't see why."

She thought for a long moment and finally said, "If they want to know how many angels there are, how they going to do it, Fynn, how?"

"Don't know, sweetie. I just have no idea. I'm sure they manage to figure it out some way."

She wasn't very impressed with that answer,

so she tried it a different way.

"Well, then," she said, "how do they know how many people they have to look after? How do they count, Fynn? How, eh?"

"Suppose they do it the same way you do. I reckon they count on their fingers."

"Pooh!" was her reply. "Angels don't have no fingers."

We were getting nowhere very fast with this kind of a conversation, so it was about time it stopped.

"Well," I ended up hopefully, "I guess they just have to count on their feathers." I realized as soon as I said it that it was a daft thing to say and I wished that I hadn't said it. She gave me one of her sad, pathetic looks and hurled another question at me.

"How many feathers they got then?"

"No idea," I replied, "I guess it must run into thousands."

"Must be funny kinds of sums then."

"I reckon it must be," I replied.

Perhaps she realized that I was teasing her for, as usual, she ended up trapping me into doing something that I had no idea how to go about.

"Fynn, can you work out how angels do sums and Mister God too and those things out there."

"Oi! Hold your horses! What things out

there? Maybe there ain't things out there."

That was a complete waste of time.

"But if there are, how do they count, Fynn? How do everything count? Can't you work it out, Fynn, and then you can tell me." It looked as though she was giving me a permanent task.

I didn't give very much thought to the angels and their sums. If they really wanted to do sums, they could work it out for themselves. Except for Anna's constant reminder,

I would have forgotten it altogether. Anyhow, up to meeting her, I had never met an angel, at least not to my knowledge, and as for Martians and other such creatures, I was completely certain I had never met any. But I did manage to work something out for her. Something that pleased her. Something that excited her. It was so obvious when I had finished it, but with no calculator or computer around then, it was a very dreary and tiresome business with all that long division.

Suppose that there is some angel or something out there with seven fingers to count on, all you do is to divide whatever number of fingers it had got, or whatever it counted on, by itself, like if it has seven fingers, divide seven by seven and of course, that's one. Then you have to divide 1 by the number of fingers. 1 divided by 7 is 0.142857142 and that is the magic number for seven fingers: 0.142857142. After that it's simple, even though it does take a long time. All you need to do is to divide that magic number by itself, which is of course 1, then you divide 1 by the magic number and that gives the answer 7. Then divide the 7 by the magic number, which takes you to 49. Then divide the number 49 by the magic number and that's 343 and then just keep on going $\times \ldots \times^2 \ldots \times^3 \ldots \times^{00}$. Every number has its own "magic number." Just another case of turning things upside down. Good old God, he's done it again! For Anna, God was just fun — sheer enjoyment.

Anna's excursion into the Bible concordance and dictionaries wasn't always a great success. The words she most wanted just weren't there. She had looked for the word "fun" for a long time, but it was nowhere to be found. She found the word "play" all right, but it didn't seem to mean what it ought to. You could play the harlot or the mad person, but where were games and just pure fun? She very soon came to the conclusion that people in the Bible didn't really have much time for children. They always seemed to be killed off for some reason.

"Don't people like kids, Fynn?" she had asked me one evening.

"Of course they do," I replied. "As far as I'm concerned there's only one thing wrong with them."

"What, Fynn?" she asked.

"Too many darned questions!" I replied.

"Oh." She looked at me. "What's that, Fynn?"

"They never stop asking questions," I grinned at her.

She spent a lot of time looking for what she called the very important words in the

Bible; kids' words, that is, not grown-up ones. It did seem so very strange to her that when you consider just how nice Mister God was, there ought to be many more laughing words and happy words in the Bible. But she could never find just the ones she wanted. The Vicar wasn't much of a help, neither was Miss Haynes.

"You're far too young to understand," she was told. "Wait until you grow up."

"Fynn," she asked, "do everybody have to grow up before they know Mister God?"

"Don't suppose it works like that," I murmured.

"Then how does it work, Fynn? How then?"

"Well," I replied hesitantly, "I guess the Vicar meant *understand* Mister God, not *know* Mister God."

"Oh."

"Sometimes, Tich, I think it's a whole lot easier for kids to know Mister God than it is for grown ups."

"Why, Fynn?" she persisted. "Why?"

I didn't quite know the answer to that one, so I just had to make it up.

"Well," I began, "I reckon grown ups have often got so many problems of their own that they just haven't got time to . . . er . . . er . . ."

"Play?" she suggested. "Play with Mister God. Eh? Play?"

"Something like that," I said.

"Um. Grown-up people make church so, well, serious that they never have time to play, do they, Fynn?"

"I guess you're just about right on that one, luv," I replied.

"Too busy trying to earn enough money to pay the bills I guess."

Anna didn't really go much on the idea that people had no time to play with Mister God. So far as she could understand the Bible and all the church services she had attended, it was often more frightening than joyful and she lost no opportunity in saying so.

"Fynn," she said, "is that why Mister John don't like Mister God?"

"Well," I replied uncertainly, "I don't think Mister John doesn't like Mister God. It's just, well . . ." As usual I was getting into very hot water and I just didn't know how to get out of the mess I was getting into. With her usual persistence, she wasn't going to let me off the hook. These kind of questions so often left me stunned. I never quite knew which way to turn. I tried to wriggle out of them, but she never allowed me to. My problem was always how to try to explain things to her without destroying her own happiness in Mister God. I didn't realize for a long, long time that nothing that I, or for that matter, anybody else, could say could possibly destroy . . . it wasn't love, it wasn't awe, it was simply happiness. She just saw God as a being of pure fun. She talked to Mister God in the same way that she talked to me or her dear friend Bombom. She saw Mister God not in the way most people did, but simply as her best friend; the kind of friend you could just chatter with and tell a funny story to. You could show him things. Well, you could simply have a good old giggle with him. She never could understand why it was you had to creep about on tiptoes or that sort of thing when you went into church. It just wasn't her. She could well understand that you would have to do that sort of thing with very important people like Kings and Queens, but surely not with Mister God! All she wanted to do with Mister God was to throw herself at him, to explode with joy. It was this spontaneous outburst that grown-up people didn't understand and simply couldn't do. She reckoned that grown ups had just forgotten how to play and it was, as she said, "about time they bleeding well did, and Mister John bleeding well didn't."

I did try to explain to Anna that it wasn't

anything to do with not liking Mister God. It was . . . it was that John just didn't believe that there was a God to like or not to like. He was totally convinced that, given a few more years, the scientists would be able to explain everything in the universe. Trying to explain this kind of thought was going to be a bit more than I could manage. But she accepted this like a duck takes to water.

It was some days later that she returned to this matter. I was just about to tuck into my favourite supper of sausages and mash when the fork I was lifting to my mouth was halted in mid-flight by her hand.

"Fynn," she said, "you know why, don't you?"

"I know why what?" I managed to say, sneaking a quick mouthful.

"Why Mister John don't believe Mister God is there."

I nearly said, "Where's there?" but I didn't. I took another quick mouthful instead. I managed to say, "No idea, Tich. Why doesn't he believe that Mister God is there?"

She gave me one of her impish grins of delight.

" 'Cos he wants to know how it all started."

"Oh, I see, that accounts for it! Don't you, then?"

She waggled her head. "No," she said. "It don't matter, do it?"

I just had to ask the next question. "What do you want to know then?"

"How it all ends and how me and you end!"

It was a great puzzle to her. The mistake people made thinking they looked like Mister God. You end up with a patchwork quilt of a God, maybe black or white, red or yellow, and possibly some other colour, she hadn't figured out. And then, of course, did it mean that Mister God was tall or short, fat or thin? This image stuff was far too dangerous to play about with. You never knew what you might end up with. If it meant anything at all, it must mean inside not outside, even that wasn't all that important. The really important thing was that he could do what we expected he could do and that was, for Anna, all there was to it.

Anna never did quite understand what all the fuss was about or why it was that some people just could not believe that God was around. So far as she was concerned, it was a stone-bonking certainty. She was sure that it was because of those words in the Bible, the bit where Mister God says, "Let us make man in our own image." That's where it all went wrong. She knew a lot about images. The circus had revealed her as a short, fat dwarf or a tall, thin giant in the distorted mirrors. Images could lead you into all sorts of trouble and, after all, Mister God never did say if he was making us in his outside image or his inside image and, since nobody had ever seen him, how do we know what he looks like? As far as she was concerned he could look like a pussy cat if he wanted to, or even a sausage roll, it was us that insisted that we looked like he did and that was what got us all mixed up. So none of that stuff was for her!

One evening we bumped into Old Woody and the night people.

"He! He! He!" he chortled. "If it isn't the little darlin' herself! Sit yerself by me, my little one, and get yerself warm. Good evening little Miss er . . . er . . ."

"It's Anna," she said.

"Anna, of course. Little Miss Anna. The little lady whose name is the same backwards or forwards. How could I forget that? Have you found all your answers yet?"

"No," replied Anna, "not yet. Some, but not very many!"

"You mustn't fret about that. None of us finds many answers. Some of us none at all."

Anna stood before Old Woody and said, "Mister, can I ask you a question?"

"Of course you may, my dear. Ask away."

She warmed her hand before the fire and said, "Mister, wot's religion? Is it about Mister God?"

"Now that is a very, very big question and I don't think anybody really knows the answer to that."

"But is it really about Mister God?"

"Hark at that!" chortled convict Bill from downunder. "That's got you stumped. Pass the bottle over!"

"Well," said Old Woody thoughtfully, "I don't really think it is all that much about God. It's about something different."

"Wot?"

"It's about an appointment that none of us have made. It was made for us."

"Oh? Where we got to go to?"

"That's another question I can't give an answer to. It might be here, it might be there, but I'm certain we will know when we get there."

"And will we see Mister God when we get there?"

"That's what I think," replied Woody. "He was the one that made the appointment. An appointment in time or space. I know not where, neither do I care, but it's there."

I liked the idea of an appointment that I had never made, and knew that I would stop being asked questions. Sure, she would collect a lot of rubbish, but I didn't want her to miss the gems. Nor did I! Fair gems are only found in the dust.

"Little Miss Anna, did you find your answer as to what poetry is?"

"Yes, Mister. Fynn's Mummy told me."

"And what did she say? Will you tell me?"

"It's the least said the better. That's what Fynn's Mummy said."

"I like the sound of that, I do indeed! 'The least said the better.' Fynn's Mummy does sound a very nice lady."

"She is," said Anna.

"But who is Fynn?"

"He," she replied, holding my hand.

"He's a lucky man."

I nodded happily. "I know I am!"

Anna's schooling never did go along with that calm and easy rhythm that most teachers wanted, but her education had taken wings long before I had ever met her. As Miss Haynes once told me, "She always gets good marks but she never seems to pay attention to what I am saying."

I wanted to tell Miss Haynes that she probably paid too much attention to what she was saying. But that would never do. Anna had looked up the word "school" in my dictionary long ago: "A place for the education of the young and a place where horses were trained." As she wasn't a horse and certainly didn't want to be instructed, she didn't want to go to school. She'd rather find out for herself. School was a bit of a bore. As far as Anna was concerned, brains was the kind of stuff you could buy in the butcher's shop or, if you were lucky, have on toast for tea. Many of the old ladies firmly believed that the more brains you could eat, the cleverer you would become. And when Miss Haynes persisted in telling her to use her brains, Anna was more than a little suspicious. So far as she was concerned, the heart was the important thing, not the brains. It was, for her, very simple. She could easily accept

that brains could find out things, but the heart was something else altogether: "That makes you understand things, don't it, Fynn?" The whole business of brains caused me no end of trouble.

"No, dear, you won't grow up to look like a sheep if you eat sheep's brains, nor a cow, nor a pig either."

"Will I get cleverer if I eat them brains, Fynn?"

That was another thing I didn't know about, but Anna could make it all sound so simple. She had no difficulty in accepting that eyes, ears and noses and the other sense organs are what puts stuff *into* your brain, and she was equally certain that the *heart* was what you used to get it *out* again when you wanted to look at it. Poor Miss Haynes! Ideas about some things got "Poohed" out of existence, and she lost about five points on that one, but then she was always losing points. Pity she didn't know it. Not that John did much better either. He was always losing points. It was comforting to know that I didn't lose as many points as either Miss Haynes or John. I lost some, but not as many as they did. What Miss Haynes and John simply did not understand was that it was all very well sticking stuff into the old brain box; the real problem was how to get it out again. You did so often tend to lose the important stuff, things that you ought to be able to find, but where were they? As Mum so often told us, "If you haven't stopped during the course of the day, you haven't done anything worthwhile." As somebody or other has said:

What is this life if full of care
We have no time to stand and stare?

Mum was never against learning or education except, as she would say, "Too much learning makes people lose heart" and, for her, losing heart was the greatest tragedy of all. Whatever else I might say about Mum and Anna, that's one thing they never did. They never lost heart. It was stopping and looking again that did the trick for them. A trick that I hadn't quite mastered.

I did enjoy the cool wind of John's approach to things, but I also enjoyed the warmer breeze of Anna's innocence. As far as I could see, the only way to go on was to accept both sides and get on with it. At least I wasn't the only person in the world to be fuddled with life! It wasn't the thought of all this extra learning that she was going to get that finally persuaded Anna. Rather, it was when John had said that on some days her friends Bombom and May could come with her in the long school holidays. After forty years of teaching, John had got the strange idea that children's minds were for filling up. He seemed to think that her habit of standing with her hands on her hips and head tilted to one side and red hair streaming, was a sign that she was ready for more facts to be poured in. I really did try to tell him that the real reason was so that the things that she didn't want to know could pour out! But he didn't believe me. He'd just have to find out for himself. Miss Haynes had tried long enough, goodness knows, and all she managed to get was a lot more grey hairs! My idea was to let Anna have a taste of everything in her own time. We had been to synagogues, churches and various kinds of chapels, and wherever we went there was always somebody who could tell you exactly what God was, what he was thinking and exactly what he wanted; and many of the books in the library weren't all that much help either.

People seemed to know everything there was to know about Mister God and then promptly forgot about it. It was all very strange. She really wanted to find out for herself. And I really should have told John that almost everything was either a "thingy," a "wotsit" or a "doings," but that was another thing I forgot.

I made her one of those devices that spun on its axis and made a series of still pictures look as if they were in motion. The book called it Phanakistoscope, and as it was difficult to ask your friends if they would like to see your Phanakistoscope, it ended up being called a "thingy"; and everybody knew exactly what a "thingy" was except, of course, the Teachers.

I always seemed to be making something or other for her, and I did wonder how John was going to manage on her continuous cloudburst of questions and answers. It was all very well if you could live underwater! I reckon some of Anna's Teachers simply got washed away in a flood of "Why?", "Where?", "What?" It wasn't always possible for her to put her ideas into words. I often had to make guesses about things until she told me I had got it right. And that isn't the kind of thing most people have got time for. Things were altogether simple for Anna; understanding something was when you could play with it. "Like Mister God," she told me. He was always ready to play hide and seek, blind man's buff and all that kind of thing. He'd just creep up behind you and ask the question, "Guess who?" The fact that at many times he could look like a tree, or a cat, or even a Phanakistoscope was really neither here nor there. You may not always know where Mister God was, but there was one thing that she was certain of, that he always knew where she was, and that was enough for her. Mum put the whole thing in a nutshell when she told John, in her own doughnut speech, "She's really not looking for a needle in a haystack, you know. It's more like she's looking for a haystack in a needle." You can't always work that kind of thing out instantly. It takes a time before it makes sense and I reckoned that was where John might have a bit of trouble.

It always gave me great pleasure to see John and Anna together — the old 'un and the young 'un. After the initial hesitation they had struck up a deep friendship. It didn't make my life any easier. In fact, it made it a darn sight more complicated, but that was fine with me. One of the problems was the fact that whatever Anna wanted to say or do, she said it in the simplest and most direct way possible. "I want to have a pee, Fynn, a piddle, a piss." It was all the same to her. I suppose it was a question of age and upbringing, but it was a lot different to John's, "Fynn, I need to relieve myself." John would so often hide what he wanted to say behind some Latin phrase or in some other language. So it meant that I had to speak two languages, his and hers; and on many occasions, act as an interpreter. It wasn't that I couldn't understand either of them, that was simple enough, but

understanding them both together, that could be a bit tough at times! Most times, I was able to listen and understand John and Anna well enough, even though it might be a bit of a struggle. It was when they got together that I so often found myself in a flat spin. Like a spectator at a tennis match, my head was going from left to right, from right to left. Normally I could manage it. The problem was when my head was going right at the same time as my eyes were going left, that caused me confusion. I wasn't made to do that kind of thing and I complained, but they both ignored my complaints. There was John who maintained that the things that mattered were the things we knew, the public things. Anna reckoned the only things that really mattered were the things we didn't know, the private things. Me? Sorry, I'm a stranger here!

As usual it was Mum who gave me the clue I needed. She told me that Mister John needed to know the biggest part and Anna wanted to know the smallest part. Put like that it made sense. After all, what do you expect from the sort of Mum who worked a sampler, as a young girl, which read "Too much of anything kills the joys of having enough." It hung over her large brass bedstead. I had learnt that she would never have had the usual sentences like "Jesus loves me" or "Bless this house." When you come to think about her sampler, it makes sense and it worked out with John and Anna too. Once I had got that secret, things were a lot easier to understand.

The large telescope in John's garden impressed Anna well enough, and well, all them stars and things, you'd have to be a bit of an idiot not to wonder at it all. But it was a pity, wasn't it, that you had to squash those five or six daisies in order to do so. There were so many times when I was uncertain if I was being stretched or flattened! It's a bit difficult to put it into words, and each time I try to do so, it can sound sillier and sillier. The only way that I could put it was that while John had spent most of his life trying to fold the whole universe into a manageable packet, Anna was, in her own way, trying to unfold the daisies to fill that empty space that John was creating. I said it was too difficult to put it into words, but it was something like that. All this reminded me of the story of, I think, the Rev. Sidney Smith, who said to his Bishop, "Is it not strange, my Lord Bishop, that you, because of your gravity, will ascend to heaven, whilst I, because of my levity, will descend to hell." For I felt suspended in the middle, going up and down like a yo-yo!

When I repeated this one afternoon John's response had been, "Are you sure it was Sidney Smith who said that, Fynn?"

"I'm not sure that it was!"

Anna thought that it was worth a snigger but really not all that important. But me, I thought it was good and I knew that somebody had said it. And it certainly wasn't me and I don't think it mattered anyway. It doesn't to me. I don't give a fig who said it. It had been said and that was good enough for me.

And then there were mirrors. I use them when I shave, but I had spent hours and hours with John learning about geometry and mathematics of single and multiple mirrors, and then more and more hours learning about the magic of mirrors.

In those days I had a book entitled *The Mathematical Analysis of Knots*. So far as I was concerned a knot was what I did when I tied up my shoes or my tie, but I read that it was more than that. The simple once-over knot, called the clover knot, went one way, but its mirror image went the other way. I never realized that. The fact that the knot and its image are called an "enantiomorphic pair" was interesting. Not that I used that word very often. And then the book went on to say that "amphicheiral" meant fitting either hand, that socks were amphicheiral but on the other hand, gloves and shoes were not. Oh! Where did this "other hand" come from? That's another thing I had never noticed. I nearly gave up when I was informed that something about these knots could be expressed analytically in its simplest form by the relation that follows:

$$x = 1 \quad y = 1 \quad x = 1$$
$$y \; x \; yx = 1 \quad y = 1 \quad xyxy = 1$$
$$x = 1 \quad y = 1 \quad xy = 1 \quad !$$

I was impressed to know that this was the simplest way of expressing it!! And I was glad to know that I had learnt to tie a knot a long time before I had read the book! Otherwise I doubt if I could ever have tied up my shoes! But it reminded me so much of John and Anna. Was it just possible that they were reverse images of each other.

It was a day like any other day at home when it started. No green clouds, no manna from heaven, not a shower of pound notes to be seen anywhere, just a smiling-faced Anna with a morning cup of tea and the sound of the milkman, the train going by, the usual factory chimneys giving out the smoke and soot. As I said, it was just plain usual, absolutely nothing to raise the flags about, but it turned out to be the day when "it" happened.

I was going to do a bit of digging for John, and Anna was to come with me. I took the tandem into the street, pumped up the tyres, checked the brakes, tested the lights. Just the common or garden ordinary things. Nothing special. I had finished the digging around about lunchtime, listening to Anna's chatter. Arabella asked us to stay for lunch, so that was fine. After lunch, we sat in the sitting-room and talked about nothing in particular, Anna looking at a large picture book, Arabella busy mending something. John and I each had a pint of beer and were just idly talking about this, that and the other. Nothing of great importance, but whether trees might have any means at all of communication with each other.

"No," he had corrected me, "they don't know each other, that would be too much. They can't possibly know anything, they were not made that way."

"There might be some possibility that they could communicate with each other in some very primitive way. I wonder what they would talk about if they could?"

"The usual things, I suppose," giggled John. " 'The weather is not quite right,' 'the children are more like mother than father,' just silly normal things."

I'm certain that Anna had not heard a word of this conversation. She was far too busy with her book. Arabella paid us no attention at all. This kind of conversation was so far beneath her as to be almost out of sight. You see, normal, just plain every day normal. Anna drifted over and sat on the arm of my chair.

"Hi, Tich," I greeted her. "What's to do? All right?"

She nodded and smiled at John. She walked around the room once or twice, stood in front of me just looking, and suddenly without any warning flung herself into my arms. Of course we were alarmed. It was so unlike her, even Arabella unfroze a bit and was ready to give out with the comfort. I held Anna tight in my arms for some minutes until she wriggled free and there she stood, grinning down at me.

"You scared me, Tich," I said. "You sure you're all right?"

"I'm good, Fynn. I'm good. Just want to say something to you, that's all."

"Sure thing, luv," I answered her. "Fire away. I'm all yours."

It was then that "it" happened. The moment when that sitting-room held one very certain child and three uncomprehending grown ups. She uttered no more than fifteen ordinary words and the world seemed to stand still. All she said was, "Fynn, you have to know much more to be silent than you do to keep talking."

John looked at me in a dazed fashion. Arabella stopped her mending and stood up. "Well," she said, and nothing more. John was struck dumb.

There were no words that I could find for that moment either. I did manage to find my tongue a few minutes later, but all that I could manage to say was, "Where did you find that one from?"

"Dunno, but it's true ain't it, Fynn? Ain't it true?"

"Suppose it must have come from one of the people she's always pestering to write it down big. I can't see how else she could have put that sentence together." And I never did find out how she came by it. Perhaps she worked it out. I just don't know. I do know that John never ceased to quote it to people. It had a profound effect on him. "It was then that it changed," he would say.

As most of Anna's little stories and her workings out were done sitting on my lap or when she had gone to bed, I knew them all by heart. Most of them had a little sting in them somewhere, but not everybody saw it. It was after we had finished tea one afternoon when John said, "Will you tell me a story, little one? I have heard a lot about your stories."

"Yes, Mister John. What one shall I tell you?"

"Whichever one you like."

"Would you like me to tell you about the

mice, or the one about heaven?"

"I think," he said, "the one about the mice would do very well. You can tell me the one about heaven another day."

"Say when you're ready then, Mister John, and then I'll start."

"I'm ready, Anna, so you may start."

"This king," she began, "had lots and lots of jewels and crowns and things like that. Then one day the biggest diamond of all fell out on the floor but nobody could ever find it again. The queen couldn't find it and the princess couldn't find it. Just nobody could find it, so in the end they all had to go to bed. Now in the middle of the night, a little mouse was looking for something to eat and he saw this diamond where nobody could find it and he tried to push it to the hole where he lived, but he couldn't move it a bit. So then he went to find his friend to come and help him, and they pushed and pushed and pushed and they couldn't do it. So they went to get some more friends to help too, but they still couldn't move it. So they called for some more friends to come and then there were hundreds of mice, all pushing this diamond and in the end it started to move and they all pushed all night long and in the end they pushed it down a hole and nobody ever saw it again. It was lost for ever."

"I see," said John, "so that is the end of that little story, is it?"

"No, Mister John. That's only the start of it. I haven't finished yet. You've got to wait for the end of the story and I haven't got there yet!"

"I'm sorry, Anna," he said a little abashed, "perhaps I'm a little too impatient."

Her "Yes, Mister John," turned him a deep crimson.

"Please go on."

"Well then, the mouses couldn't find it either, 'cos it had fallen down a very deep hole and they couldn't get down it. Then, Mister John, one of the mice said to the first mouse, 'What did we all push it for?' And do you know, Mister John, nobody could tell why they had worked so hard! Nobody could say why they did it at all! You couldn't eat it, could you? And nobody knew what you could do with it. It was a very silly thing for all them mouses to do, wasn't it, Mister John? And it was only because a king wanted to look important first of all. And that's the end of the story of all them silly mouses. But it's like people too, ain't it, Fynn?"

I was used to being given the hard bits to sort out afterwards, so I was ready for any question that John might ask. I think he got lost with all those mice dashing about, for he never said a word until Anna had gone out into the garden.

"I suppose, Fynn, she's saying that many people do useless things and have no idea why they are doing them. Is that it?"

"You said it, John, not me," I laughed.

"Then why didn't she talk about people not mice?"

"Perhaps, John, if she had talked about people, you might not have believed her. It's a lot easier to believe mice are silly, rather than people."

"Perhaps you're right, Fynn. I really must wait for the end of stories, mustn't I?"

Of all the odd jobs I did in my spare time, the one I enjoyed the most was driving the Baker's horse and van back to the depot, little more than four miles away, and I could earn anything between two shillings and sixpence and four shillings a time. Money for old rope. There was nothing difficult in driving Old Tom. He knew his way home better than I did. On some occasions, when the driver, after a night out, didn't feel up to it, I did take on the whole round. I could make as much as 12/6d for that, which wasn't bad going. Tom was so certain of the delivery round that he always stopped at the right pavement. With both front legs on the pavement and

neck outstretched he waited for his titbit, a nob of sugar, a carrot or an old stale bun. He would not move until he had been given it. If Tom had been able to count money, I would have been out of a job. I often told him he was just an old flea-bag, but he didn't understand me, or if he did, he took no notice. He was living in clover with all these extras and he got all the pats and strokes. Nobody ever did that to me. His attitude to me sometimes made me feel quite useless. Fred had told me often enough, but somehow I always forgot when the time came. "Never turn your back on him, that's the one thing he doesn't like." I could take his harness off, give him a brush down, feed him and water him and then turn away to lock the stall. He'd put his head in the small of my back and, with a twist and a shove, send me flying across the stable. If he had any sense maybe I could have reasoned with him, but he never could understand me, not even when I called him a flea-bag. That dratted horse could make me feel so small at times, especially when the others laughed at the number of times he bowled me over.

There was one November day when I was certain that my shrinkage was beginning to show. We had one of those November fogs, not the ordinary ones, but a "peasouper," those fogs when you took two steps outside your front door and were immediately lost. Nobody could see the street names and the street lights were nothing more than a greenish fuzz. It wasn't that you couldn't see your hand in front of your face, you just couldn't see it anywhere. This particular evening it was so thick that you could have nailed a plank of wood to it, or leant a ladder against it and climbed it. Some of the kids could make a few pennies on nights like this. With a paraffin lamp they could walk the curb directing a lost bus or a lonely car or two. Nobody knew where they were.

"Am I all right for the Broadway, mate?"

"Don't know, chum, I think it's the other way, but I'm not sure."

Eventually I did find my way back home.

"What a night!" I complained to Mum. "It's a real stinker!"

"Glad I'm in. It's not a night to be out."

"What's for supper, Mum? I'm just about ready for it."

"Fred Cooper's not well," she said. "He's got bronchitis. Can you take the van back to the yard for him?"

"Right," I said, "but I must have a cup of tea first and I'd better put something warmer on."

"His Missus left something for your trouble."

She had left me five shillings.

"No trouble, Mum," I said. "Buy yourself a tiara or something."

"A couple of bags of coal would be nice," she replied. "What with the winter coming on that'll be right handy."

"Good idea. I'll put it behind the clock for you."

"Can I come with you, Fynn?" asked Anna.

"That's fine with me, but you'd better ask Mum."

"Well," said Mum, "as long as you keep warm and don't do anything silly, yes."

"How will you manage to get home if it's as thick as all that?" Mum called after us up the passage.

"Don't worry about that, Mum," I said. "We'll sleep with the horses if it doesn't clear soon. They won't mind."

"Right," she replied. "I'll see you when I see you. Take care!"

We closed the street door and headed up the street. The fog was just as bad as it had been an hour ago.

"Can Bombom come?" asked Anna.

"If she wants to, of course, she can."

In a few minutes, I was joined at the top of the street by Bombom, May, Nipper and

Anna. Millie was by the lamppost talking to a couple of her friends.

"Where you lot off to?" she asked. "Taking Fred's van back to the yard for him? He's got his chest again."

"Like to come for a ride, Mill? You might not get back till the morning and if it goes on like this, you'll have to sleep with the horses."

"I'm game. Lead on."

In no time at all we were outside Fred's house.

"I'll just pop in to have a word with Fred. You might as well put Tom's nosebag on until I get back."

"He can't go out on a night like this, Fynn. It'll kill him," said Mrs Fred.

"Thanks for taking Tom back for me," said Fred when I went in. "Perhaps you'll do my round for me in the morning if I don't get in."

"Sure I will. You get some rest."

"Tom will see you back safely."

"Right, Fred. I'd better go now. I've got a van load of kids waiting for me."

"That's good. It'll be company for you. Oh Fynn, there's cold pies in the locker. You might just eat them between you."

Outside the kids were waiting for me.

"Fynn," laughed Millie, "we've got a lost

Copper who wants a lift to the station. Any chance? It's PC Laithwaite."

We moved back the way we had come and I stopped the van next to the King's Head. "Gonna buy some fizz," I said. "Back in a tick."

As I clambered back onto the seat, I heard a lady say, "I didn't know it was going to be like this, did I?"

"Now we are in a fix," came the man's voice. "I can't possibly drive the car back in this."

"That's Mister John, Tich," I whispered to Anna. "Hop down and tell him."

"Hello, Mister John," I heard her say.

"Well bless me. It's the little maid herself. Are you lost too?"

"No, Mister John."

"We are and I don't see any way of getting back."

"Ask Fynn. He can do it for you."

"Fynn! Where is he?"

"Up here, John," I laughed. "Would you like a lift home? I'm going your way."

"Oh Fynn, could you really find your way in this?"

"Not me," I replied, "but Old Tom can."

It was arranged that Danny would drive John's car back, following Old Tom and the van. Arabella wasn't at all certain that she was ever going to get home again and, as for sitting behind a smelly old horse, well "the indignity of it!" Anna did manage to tell her that even the King and Queen did that kind of thing. She started to tell us that riding in a coach with smart horses pulling it was one thing, Old Tom and the Baker's van was something entirely different. We did at last manage to convince her that it was Tom and the van or nothing. She wasn't certain that I could manage either: "I must sit with my back to the horse. I really couldn't bear to watch." I told her that I couldn't see either, and that didn't help a bit. The fact that she would have to rely on a mere horse, a dumb animal, to get her home was almost too much for her.

At last we managed to get away, Old Tom plodding his steady way along the road. There was nothing much I could really do, with Anna beside me on the box and the rest of the passengers packed in the van. I asked Anna to get a cigarette from my pocket and lit it. When Arabella saw that I wasn't holding the reins in my hand, she nearly had the vapours.

"Fynn, do be careful. Don't let it run away!"

"Run, Arabella? Old Tom hasn't run for the last ten years. He's got too much sense for that."

Poor Arabella, for all her learning, really

didn't know very much about ordinary things like the way Old Tom was clever at cutting across the tramlines, which could be a little tricky at times. I never managed to work out exactly how he did that, but I never knew him to make a mistake except on the one occasion some time ago when I had pulled the rein too much. That was the time when I nearly had the van over, but since then I just let him get on with it at his own pace.

PC Laithwaite dropped off at the Station House without my needing to stop. I asked Millie where the cold pies were to be found, but Arabella would have none of it.

"Is Danny still with us?" I asked.

"Yes, Fynn," said Bombom, her mouth full of pie. "Fynn!"

"Yes?"

"Can I come and sit between you and Anna?"

"Sure thing. Just clamber up."

She hadn't been with us for more than a minute or two when Tom came to a stop.

"Fynn," Bombom said, "now the horse is lost too."

"Is he lost, Fynn? Do you know where we are yet?" Arabella piped up.

"He's having a drink," Bombom told her.

"What's that noise?" asked Arabella.

"He's having a pee too," explained Anna. Now I knew exactly where we were — the horse trough by the canal bridge. We weren't doing badly at all. We ought to make it in about thirty minutes.

As we travelled westwards away from all the factories, the fog thinned out just a bit. Not that I could see all that much better, but at least the street lamps no longer had that greenish tint to them, and it wasn't too long before I pulled Tom to a stop.

"Where are we now?" Arabella asked.

"Home, Arabella. Safe and sound."

She could hardly believe it was true. I had to refuse her invitation for a hot drink. She was a little surprised when I told her that we couldn't stop, for it was about time Old Tom was tucked up in bed. For John and Arabella all animals were dumb creatures. She didn't want to believe that it was Tom who had got her home safely, dumb or not.

We made it to the stables in less than fifteen minutes. The fog here had lifted considerably. I took the harness off and wiped it down, gave Tom a good brush down and instructed Millie and the kids how to find his food and water and just where to put them. Then I led Tom to his stall. I was very careful not to turn my back on him that night, but I think he had had enough of that day and didn't give me any trouble at all. It didn't take us long to make up a comfortable bed for the night.

Armfuls of hay, a number of horse blankets and the odd bag of oats, and we were ready for sleep. Even Anna was reduced to a sentence or two.

"Fynn, Jesus was born in a place like this, wasn't he?"

"Don't think it was as nice as this," I yawned.

"Oh, don't suppose so." A little chorus of good nights were exchanged and I think the last thing I remembered was her "Good night, Mister God."

I woke up next morning with somebody trying to poke my brains out with a straw in my ear. "Hi, Fynn, time to wake up!"

"Millie, what's to do? Stop poking my ear, will you? Where have the kids got to?"

Peals of laughter from outside in the van yard told me all I wanted to know. "What day is it, Millie?"

"Saturday . . . all day long."

"That's something," I said. "Any idea what the time is?"

"Just after six. The church clock just struck."

"Suppose we'd better get a move on then. Has Fred been in?"

"Haven't seen anybody at all."

"Give me a hand, Millie. I'm stuck."

With her help I got to my feet. So far as

I could figure it out, I had only stopped for five or six hours out of the last thirty-six. I was a bit washed out.

The foreman and a couple of ladies were in the yard with the kids, who were filling themselves with cakes and tea.

"Thanks for bringing the van back. There weren't all that many who made it last night. A regular stinker wasn't it? I've had a message from Fred. He says if you can do his round for him today he can bring the van back tonight. The fog has cleared up nicely and it looks like it's going to be a nice day. I've made the Saturday book up for you, and your young helpers are packing the van now. Perhaps you had better look it over so that you know where the stuff is." He slipped a ten shilling note into my hand. "Thanks," he said, "once again."

"I must have a drink and a bite before we set off."

"Mary," he called, "you can bring the young lady too."

Millie arrived looking spic and span as usual. "Surprising what a lick of powder and paint can do for a girl, ain't it, Fynn?"

"You look all right to me without it."

"Thanks, Fynn. Don't stop, tell me more! You'll get yourself a bad name one of these days, Fynn."

"How come?" I asked her.

"If the street ever gets to hear that you spent the night in bed with four young ladies, your name will be mud!"

The name of John's house, Random Cottage, had puzzled Anna for a long time. It didn't seem to mean anything at all. If it had been called "The Larches" or "Hill View" or something like that, that would have been fine. She could have understood that. But "Random," I ask you! What did that mean? She told me that the very next time she saw John, she was going to ask him why.

I had been puzzling my head all week long over some bit of mathematics that I could not understand. Come Sunday afternoon I decided I was going over to see John before my head finally came off its hinges. Anna was off somewhere playing with her friends. Going to John and back certainly wouldn't take more than a couple of hours and I'd be back before supper. I would sneak off while she was busy. The street was full of kids playing their various games. As I made my way to the top of the street, "Game of cricket, Fynn?" asked Heck.

"Not now. Going to be busy for an hour or so." I had to dodge the skippers, the gobstone players and the odd ball players. I had almost made it to the top of the street when I was nearly knocked flying by Anna.

"Where are you going, Fynn? Going to John D.? Going on yer bike?"

"Not this time. Going to run along the canal. See you in a few hours' time, Tich."

I ran slowly the last few yards to the top of the street and I was just about to turn the corner and head for the canal when the quick patter of feet pulled me up short, to say nothing of the persistent cries of "Fynn, Fynn." Two young bodies thumped into me, Anna and Bombom.

"Fynn," said Anna, "why is it called that?"

"Why's what called what?"

"Mister John's house, why is it called that?"

"I don't know. You'd better ask him when you see him next."

"You ask him," said Bombom.

"What's it mean, Fynn? What's it mean?"

"Tell you when I get back," and I started off again.

"Meany," said Anna. "Fynn's an old meany."

After the space of a breath or two Bombom joined in the chorus. The two of them ran after me with their chorus of "Fynn's a meany, Fynn's an old meany." I could have got away from them quite easily except that I was hailed by Millie.

"Hi, Fynn, what's to do? Pinched the kids' sweets again?"

"Where did that idea come from?" I asked.

"The way you're being chased," she gestured with her arms.

I turned to look. They hurled themselves at me. Being caught off balance I ended up none too elegantly or gently face down in the road. I really could have got up except for Millie's foot which pressed me flat again. If nothing else, I was now looking upwards, not with a face full of gravel.

"There, there, Fynn. You'd better have a rest and get your breath back! Can't have the old 'uns too excited now, can we?"

My intention was to chase after her, but with her foot firmly on my nose pressing me back, it was difficult for me to do anything as she counted "6-7-8-9-OUT."

"You'd better give up, Fynn. You'll never win with the kind of kids you run around with."

By this time I was encircled by faces looking down at me.

"You kids mustn't bully Fynn, you know. He's not as young as he used to be. What's he been up to? Pinched your lollies or summat?"

"He won't do something for me, that's what!" said Anna. "He's a meany!"

"May you be forgiven, you little perisher!" I managed to say before Millie's foot pushed me back again.

"Ask him again, Anna," giggled Millie, "ask him while he's helpless. The way he's going on he'll probably never get back today. Get knocked over by a train or something. Go on, ask him again. I'll hold him still," and she applied a little more pressure to my face. "Ask him while he can still breathe."

It was just another one of those occasions that I wasn't going to get out of. I had better make the best of it. What the passersby thought of this little episode, I don't know. I didn't get any help. I was a little anxious when the large dog joined the circle and then happily went off in search of his favourite lamppost.

"Come on, Anna, ask the question. Fynn's coming back to life."

"Fynn." She spoke my name in that kind of apologetic melody that only children who know they are on to a sure thing can manage.

"Mercy, I give up! What means what?"

"That 'Random' word. That's what's what. What does it mean? Ask him!"

"O.K. Mill, lift the foot and let me up."

"Always told you it was no good trying to be a genius. You'll come to a sticky end if you go on like that, Fynn." I didn't think that

John would mind my telling him that he never had this kind of problem — when I got there!

On my feet at last I made threatening signs at Millie, a promise to strangle her.

"No violence, please Fynn. Only trying to spread a little light on things. Wouldn't mind knowing what it means myself. Give with the wisdom, what does it mean?"

"Well, it's a sort of . . . it's a kind of muddle, I guess. Sort of no shape to it."

"Gawd blimey, Fynn! What, you mean it's a lot of fuss about nothing?

"Ain't intelligence wonderful?" she said to the world at large.

It wasn't exactly what I had wanted to say. It really needed a little more thought.

Lying with my face pressed into the gravel, I had got a gleam of an idea. "Don't worry, Tich, I'll ask Mister John and I'll tell you what he says when I get back."

"Oh no you don't! You can't wriggle out of it all that easy. It's now or you don't go!"

"Yes, master. The genie of the handbag is now about to do its stuff! That's if I can find the darn thing. Where did that darn pen go to? Never can find the blessed thing when I want it."

It was Bill who spotted it first, plunged his hand into Millie's bag and produced the fountain pen. I took a peek into the handbag.

"Cripes, what's all this junk for? You could start a shop with this lot."

"You stick to what you think you know, genius, and keep your nose out of my bag. It's got nothing to do with you. Ain't that right, kids?"

"What about a sheet of paper then? And you might as well dig out the table and chair too while you're about it!"

She swung her handbag at me but missed, which was a good thing considering all the stuff she had got in it.

"Paper," I demanded. "Paper."

She took a bag of apples out of her other shopping bag and handed them around and gave me the bag.

"Don't I get one?"

"Not till after. If I can understand what you're going on about, you might."

I shook the pen vigorously over the paper bag, which was soon covered by a multitude of spots. "That," I said, handing the bag around, "is random, well more or less. It gives you the idea. There is no real order. It's kind of messy. There is nothing much you can say about it."

"Bet that took a long time to figure out, Fynn!" Millie said.

"Couldn't do it meself! Takes brains that does! I'm just a dummy! Thrilling. That's what it is! Reckon I won't sleep for weeks after all that excitement! Takes real brains to do something you can't talk about! You must do it more often! Give your brains a rest!"

"Moron," I yelled over my shoulder as I fled.

I decided to anticipate her, and more than an hour later I reached Random Cottage. After I had explained the reason and asked Anna's question, he answered with, "Just luck. Nothing more than that. One of those long lost relations that fairy stories tell you about. Nothing more. I was very lucky. It's as simple as that. It was a whim, a fancy, that made me give it the name 'Random.' Odd, isn't it?" he continued, looking around the house. "It pleases me to call it that. There is nothing that I can say about the word. Chance, nothing more." Everything in his house and garden was so well ordered that the word "random" was a joke, and he smiled whenever he used it. When I returned home, that paper bag with all its dots was spread out on the table with Anna's head down over it. I told her of the conversation I had had with John and got nothing more than "Oh."

"That's the last of that," I thought. Little did I know how wrong I was! For after a few days, that paperbag with its dots was now a large sheet of white cardboard with even more dots. Except for the occasional, "You can't say a fink about it," which could have meant anything, nothing more was said for a while. I was nearly trapped into asking her what it was that you couldn't say anything about. I didn't because there was no use messing about asking silly questions if I didn't know what she was on about. After the umpteenth time of hearing that "you could say nothing about it," it was about time to ask my question.

"Sorry, Tich, no idea what you're talking about. What you on about?"

"You know, Mister John's house."

"Random Cottage?"

She nodded. "You know, you said you couldn't say much. You know, about the word 'random'."

"You mean that one?"

"Well . . ." when she said "well" in that way it was about time to duck. She darted to the cupboard and pulled out the large sheet of white cardboard which was now covered with circles and a few coloured dots. After a time to get her thoughts sorted out, she stabbed the red dot with her finger: "That's you, Fynn, that is."

"Oh, I see. Can't I be something important for a change? Something vital?"

"It is, Fynn. It is something important. And

that's me," pointing to a blue dot.

"Nice to have a bit of company. I was beginning to get a bit lonely." Her smile was comforting, but the sharp intake of her breath meant that I was getting a bit too frivolous. This wasn't the time to be funny. This was going to be serious stuff. She moved to the Welsh Dresser and got my best brass geometry set. Nobody else would dare do such a thing. That was strictly hands off! Whatever it was that she was going to say was obviously so important that she didn't ask. She just looked at me. I did nod, but that was just for the sake of appearance. Sitting opposite me she opened the lid. Her hand hesitated and she gave me that look — the look of something important to come. "Can I, Fynn? Can I?"

I nodded. She drew out the largest compass in the box, the one with the extending legs. After waving it about like the sword Excalibur and carefully inspecting the point with that air of concentration and revelation to come, she turned her gaze on me. "This," I thought, "is going to be good."

"Fynn," she said, pointing at the red dot again, "that's you."

"I know, you told me."

And with that, she stuck the point of the compass in me, the red dot I mean. I couldn't help it, it just came out. "Oi! That hurts!" That remark wasn't worth noticing. She was busy opening the compass until the writing point met one of the dots, and with the sharp bit still stuck in me, the red dot, she drew a circle. So far so good. It was more than an hour before she had finished doing the same thing for each one of the other dots and there I was, right in the centre of all those concentric circles. It was about time she recognized how important I was, but she hadn't finished yet!

"Fynn, all the other dots want it too. They want them circles too."

It was a funny thing how Anna's dots or blobs always seemed to end up being more human than humans. At least they did know what they wanted.

"I done that too! I done it! I'll go and get it!"

Yet another sheet of white card was laid on the kitchen table. It was a bit different but the point was lost on me. In this one all dots' wishes and wants had been fulfilled, for now each and every dot was firmly in the centre of its own private nest of concentric circles.

"Good, ain't it?" she asked.

"Very good," I agreed I nearly said it, but I had noticed something that I hadn't accounted for. Simple really when you think about it, but I had missed it. For one circle of every other dot passed slap bang through the middle of me. There was the dot called Anna, Mum, Millie and, since everybody is a dot, you too!

"What's all this mean, Fynn? What's it mean?"

I hesitated. The idea that was going through my head made sense to me. At least, it sounded all right, so I said it.

"What it looks like," I said, "is that every dot can be seen in two ways. Either it can be the centre of everything or" — and this was the tricky bit — "every dot is a special, no unique, meeting point of one circle of every other dot."

I got a kiss for that. I had no words for her.

"Like Mister God, ain't it? It's funny when you know how."

"Plain funny how everything is like Mister God."

"Took a long time doing it, that did."

"I bet it did!"

"Me bum went to sleep."

"It's surprising nothing else went to sleep, the way you sit."

She could always, and for that matter often did, mix God and bums and the strangest of things in one sentence, but then I really don't suppose Mister God minded at all. After all, he had been around a fairly long time.

The Rev. Castle didn't get the point and really wasn't impressed. As for John, he said, "She doesn't understand the difficulties yet. I see what she is getting at, but that is pure cheek, it's not mathematics!" He didn't understand that it wasn't meant to be mathematics. All she was trying to do was to talk about something that nobody was supposed to be able to talk about, and as far as I could see she had done just that. The idea that everything could be seen either as the centre of all things or as a unique meeting place of everything else was all right with me. I felt I could stick with that one. It was time for lots and lots of tea after that.

* * *

It wasn't that the people in the street were poverty stricken, nothing like that. It was simply the fact that they didn't always have enough money and there are plenty of disadvantages in that state of affairs. But there were a few advantages like knowing each other, helping each other, making do, the necessary inventions of living. All these things were about as normal as breathing. It was one of those things that John never fully understood. Perhaps in the long run it didn't matter one bit, except for the fact that many things had to be done another way and Anna was an expert in doing things another way. Many of her thoughts had to be seen in "the other way" and if you didn't know "the other way," it was quite easy to end up wondering what had happened and what had hit you! The Sunday that she spent the whole service drawing little circles in the air with her forefinger was one of those occasions. The Rev. Castle wasn't at all pleased with this activity and told me so, and John simply saw it as the idle doodling of the young. I was asked, no told, to do the same thing in the same direction.

She crossed the road, skirting the tram and dodging the odd horse and cart, and stood opposite me, still drawing her little circles, as I was doing. She managed to persuade some passer-by to copy her in this circle-drawing stuff and sped back to me. I was still busy drawing little circles in the air.

PC Laithwaite grinned at me. "Nice to see you occupied for a change," was all he said. He had soon got used to the fact that if Anna was around, somebody near to her was almost certain to be doing something out of the ordinary. Maybe even a little crazy. Most often me or Millie.

Miss Haynes never did understand why Anna would often stop and slowly spin around. It wasn't anything new to John. He had spent many hours talking about it, but her ideas about this circle-drawing were not the same as his. She told him quite simply and clearly that it was like being two people. He tried to give her the proper explanation, but whatever anybody else might say it was like being two people. Maybe even more than two and that was definite. After all, if on one side of the road you had to say that the circle was going one way, but on the other side of the road, that invisible circle was going the other way, of course it was like being two people! Once she asked me what a "vicious circle" was and other little gems that grown-up people talked about, like reading between the lines, which was rather daft because there wasn't anything between the lines, anybody could see that.

It wasn't often that I made the journey to Random Cottage alone, and when I did I spent more time talking about Anna than I did in the garden. John wanted to know everything she had done since he last saw her: what she had said, what her latest ideas were. Most times we arrived with her sitting on my handlebars or, if Bombom was to come with us, then we'd go by bus, and whenever the weather was fine and warm, they would sit at his feet and he'd listen to their chatter. And as he grew stronger, he would often join in their little games.

"Nothing too strenuous, John, remember what the Doctor said," Arabella reminded him.

"Bosh. Fetch me a drink, will you, Fynn, and one for yourself and find something for the children."

Since we had been going to John's house so often he was never without a plentiful supply of drinks for the children.

There were many times when I thought that Anna ought to have been born a mountain goat, the way she could jump from one subject to another which so often confused her teachers and got me into hot water. For one thing, there was this large building site up by the bridge. Everybody complained about the mess it was making, the inconvenience it caused. There were piles of bricks, pipes, planks of wood, cement, sand and a lot of rubbish too. You'd just never think to look at it that somebody knew that the mess was going to be a building at some time. That was the way she saw her schooling and all her various explorations. Some things were good and she wanted them, but others were not so good and she had no use for them. Her teachers didn't really understand, but in the end it was going to turn out to be a "Who knows?" and I was prepared to wait. It was bound to be something splendid and that was good enough for me! It was funny with grown ups, they were always throwing the most important things away. For instance, that dandelion that John had dug up.

"Can I have it please?"

"What do you want a thing like that for? There's too many of them. They are nothing but a nuisance."

That wasn't what Anna thought about them. They really ought to be somewhere nice, so she planted it in a flower bed in the park. It didn't last very long there either. And then the Rev. Castle was almost outraged to find Anna planting this dandelion in the churchyard and he told her so in no uncertain terms. It wasn't all that long ago that he was telling the congregation that God saw that it was good and she completely agreed with him. If only grown ups could have seen things as she saw them, things would have been a lot easier, but they didn't and Mum ended up with the best weed garden in the country. Surely you'd have to be a real idiot not to say that weeds were truly beautiful if they were looked after properly and it was Anna's pleasure to do so.

In spite of Miss Haynes' anguish and John's concern about her disorganized mind, she continued to look for those things that Mister God saw were good. The fact that they sometimes turned up in the most unlikely places didn't really matter at all. After all, things always grow in the cracks in the wall, on waste land and in all sorts of unlikely places, and it really wasn't right to pull them up. All things were bright and beautiful, she felt, if you only stopped to look at them. And why did we have to spoil Mister God's fun? He must have thought it was important. So Anna's ways of going about things were just that bit different. Maybe if John had been woken up in the middle of the night, as I had been so often, he might just have come to an understanding of Anna's way a lot sooner than he did. But he was woken up only once at two o'clock and

I got blamed for it. If only Anna had been able to read my night-time dreams as easily as she seemed to read my day-time thoughts, I feel sure that she wouldn't have woken me up so often. I never did get to the nice part of the dream. It would have been nice to hold all the money in my hand just for once, the money from the inheritance that the nice solicitor told me about, but that never did happen. I had to wake up to "Fynn, what's a moron?"

"Fynn, what's a moron?" she thumped me on the chest. " 'Cos Mister John said I was one."

"Not you, Tich. Maybe me, but not you."

"He did, Fynn. He said I was a moron. You've gotta tell him not to call me that. You've gotta tell him so!"

"Sure, I'll tell him the next time I see him. I sure will tell him."

"No, now Fynn. Tell him now."

"I really don't think he'd like being woken up this time of night."

"Don't care. Tell him, tell him I'm not a moron."

She sounded so near to tears that there was nothing else to do but tell him now. As we headed for the nearest telephone box I tried to convince her that he wouldn't say a thing like that.

"But he did, Fynn. He really did!"

I reckon anybody who called a little girl like Anna a moron deserved to be woken up, no matter what the hour. Anyhow, he did have a telephone next to his bed. He didn't even have to get out of bed to answer it. Not like me, I had to get dressed and walk nearly half a mile. Anna tried to get the number a couple of times and at last the operator made the connection. I pressed myself as near to the ear piece as I could. I could hear his bell ringing and very soon I heard his voice.

"Hello, John Hodge speaking."

"You do it, Fynn. You say it!"

I shook my head. "It's your fight, you do it!"

"Mister John," she bellowed down the phone, "it's Anna."

"Hello, Anna. What do you want? Are you all right? Is Fynn all right?"

"Yes, Mister John. He's here. He wants to talk to you," and with that she thrust the telephone into my hands with a little sob.

"What's all this about calling Anna a moron, John? I wouldn't do that. She says you did and she's very upset about it."

"Put her on, Fynn. For goodness sake, put her on!"

"Anna, my dear," he said, "I would never call you a moron. I couldn't do that!"

"Yes, you did, Mister John. I heard you say, 'She's the only two-legged moron that you had ever met'."

"No, no, little Anna, you have made a mistake. Not a moron, I said you were an oxymoron. Will you put Fynn on. I had better explain to him."

"Stupid men," came a voice. "You ought to know better than to frighten a little child."

"Madam, will you please get off the line. This is important."

"You bet it is," said the operator. "You both

deserve to be locked up, confusing the kid with your stupid oxy stuff. She ought to be tucked up in bed. My advice is to take her home and give her a good cuddle."

"Madam, please get off the line."

"Fynn," he said, "the word is not moron. It's oxymoron, you know, oxymoron."

Oxymoron wasn't a word I used every day of my life. It wasn't a very useful kind of word. The only time I ever remember using it was in an English lesson many years ago.

"Let's go and get a cuppa, Tich," I said. "I think we need one."

"Is it all right then, Fynn? Did he mean it?"

"He didn't say what you thought he said. He said a different word."

"What word?"

"He called you an oxymoron."

"Is that word bad, then?"

"Not really. It's what is called 'a figure of speech.' Drink your tea while it's hot."

Somewhere at the back of the old brain box I remembered an example.

"It's like when people say 'hasten slowly' or like when people say 'a living death' or something like that. It is two words that contradict each other separately, but put together make sense. It's something like that. That's what Mister John called you, not a moron."

186

"Oh," she said. "That's different. That's all right, I thought he said something else.

"Them things," she said, "you gotta be careful, ain't you, Fynn? I'm an oxymoron, ain't I, Fynn?"

She told the coffee stall owner too. "I'm an oxymoron!" I don't think he really cared a bit.

"I'm tired," I complained. "Can I go back to bed?"

I was glad that she thought it was a good idea too!

Mum called down the stairs as we got into the house.

"Where have you two been off to? It's nearly morning."

"Been killing oxymoron," I yelled back.

"That's nice," came the answer.

It wasn't until I was once again in bed that it came to me just how strange this night had been. "The pointed conjunction of seeming contradictories" was the dictionary definition of an oxymoron, so I guess John wasn't so far out after all. She was an oxymoron, sort of, and, for that matter, put together they made another one. All I was left with was the fact that "you've gotta be careful."

More and more I was getting the feel of it. Being by now so used to the way both expressed ideas, I was able to translate John to Anna in a way that she could understand, and I could do the same for John when he was finding it a bit difficult. I must confess, I often found it difficult too. Whatever it was that was so perplexing him was causing him no little pain and confusion, but one thing was for sure, he was beginning to lose that acid touch in his conversation with her; that exasperation which he had so often shown; that sharp edge in him which could hurt so often was beginning, slowly, to take on a more gentle edge. And as for Anna, she was losing none of her magic, but in some ways developing better ways of saying exactly what she wanted to. Not much, but a bit. Partly, I suppose, just because she was growing up. Poor John was really having a rough time of it. There was no sudden revelation to him, no blinding illumination. It was all a very slow progress and all with the greatest difficulty. In what direction, he did not know. For that matter neither did she and, least of all, me!

John decided that Anna ought to be given the benefit of his knowledge of things, so it was arranged that we pay a whole day's visit to the various Museums in South Kensington. I didn't like to tell him that we had already been there and that she didn't think much of them.

So it was that a little group of kids, about eight, waited for him one morning. I had asked Millie if she would come along to help out. I didn't fancy the job of chasing the kids around the Museum. She agreed.

John arrived, ready to stuff our heads full of information. In the centre of the large entrance hall to the Museum was a large model of a human flea, bigger than Anna herself. She circled it, giving it a wary glance. The shake of her head indicated that she didn't think much of it and wasn't at all interested in whatever John, or anybody else, might have to say about it. I did mention to John that they did at least have something in common, that both of them made me want to scratch something I couldn't reach, but he simply frowned at me.

After months of Anna I knew all about this need to scratch when she got going, but John hadn't learnt that yet. He would, given time. But after years of being taught by John, I wasn't going to protect him from her kind of torture. He was old enough to look after himself.

"Fynn," he asked, "has Anna been to the Hall of Dinosaurs?"

"Don't know. I don't think so."

"Well, in that case we must go along to see them. I'm certain that she will be impressed."

We saw the bronto things, the stego things, the icthyo things, and other things that nobody but John could pronounce, and finally ended up in front of good old Tyrannosaurus Rex. John poured out facts and figures about old Rex, but his millions and millions of years didn't impress any of the kids at all.

"Wouldn't like to meet him in the dark," said Millie, and Bombom's "Blimey!" exhausted her comments. May's cry of "Coo . . . ee!" echoed around that hall and turned a few heads for a moment. Well there isn't much you can say about such a thing as old Rex, is there? "Strewth!" just about sums it all up.

We moved off to look at more wonders, with John still giving out with his hundred-million-years-ago facts. I knew how easy it was to lose Anna and, for that matter, get lost myself when she was doing a bit of thinking and, as she wasn't with the rest of them, I had to go back to look for her. I found her swinging her satchel, dwarfed beneath good old Rex, all teeth and claws. From the way she was swinging her satchel and the look she gave it, her thoughts were pretty obvious. If she wasn't frightened of Old Nick himself, she certainly wasn't frightened of old Rex.

"Don't you start on me or you'll get a good slosh with me bag."

She smiled at me and wrinkled her nose as I stood beside her, and we went off in search of John and the others. When we found them, John was busy trying to convince May that this exhibit was called a Duck-billed Platypus and not a plat-billed-ducky-bus. In spite of all his insistence, it remained a plat-billed-ducky-bus for ever more!

After an hour or two it was decided that it was about time we went into the gardens to eat our sandwiches. John sat on a bench beside me, and the others on the grass. He wanted to know what Anna thought of all those dinosaurs.

"Did you like them, little one?"

"Um," she replied.

"Did they frighten you?"

She wagged her head.

"What did you think of them?"

She thought for a moment or two and, looking him straight in the eye, said, "No meat!"

It wasn't what he had expected to hear, and he launched himself into the task of telling her that the flesh had decayed millions of years ago. That didn't get much further.

"Um, I know that, Fynn told me."

He didn't know that "no meat" was important to her.

"Do you think the little maid is enjoying this, Fynn?" he asked me. "It's not too much for her, is it?"

"Don't think so, John. I'm sure she's taking most of it in."

"She seems so quiet, not like her usual self. I wondered if she was feeling unwell."

"Don't take any notice of that, John. She's thinking, that's all. Trying to put it all together, trying to work it all out. She's often like this."

"It would be nice to see inside her head for a while."

"I shouldn't try that one, John, if I were you. You'll never find your way out again and I'm not sure there's all that much space left, with all the stuff she manages to cram inside her noodle!"

"Perhaps you're right at that. The thing that really puzzles me, young Fynn, is how anyone, faced with this evidence, could possibly believe that the Bible was right. How the creation story can stand up against all these facts is beyond me."

"I don't see that the Bible tells you much. It merely creates moods."

Neither of us had noticed that Anna was standing nearby and must have heard what he had said, but she said nothing at all, nothing but a sniff.

"Will you and Millie be able to take care of the children for thirty minutes? I have a little business to attend to."

I did manage to convince him that we had done this kind of thing before and that they would be safe, even if Millie and me weren't!

"We'll be off to the Science Museum next, John. See you there in an hour or so."

"Right," he answered. "I'll find you somewhere."

The kids found this much more interesting. All those buttons to push and a whole row of historical lavatories, where they could pull the chains much better than all the dead things. Dead birds and stuffed animals were all right as far as they went, but not as much fun as the buttons that made the wheels go round, model trains, model cars and all that sort of thing. They were obviously so engaged in button-pushing that they wouldn't miss me.

"Millie, d'you mind if I lose myself for a while? I'd like to look at a display."

"Sure thing, Fynn. Where you off to?"

"Next floor up. There's a display of mathematical models I'd like to look at."

"Might have known it," she laughed. "Trust you."

I hadn't been there very long before Anna's

red hair wriggled under my arm. "Fynn."

"Hi, Tich! What's to do? Run out of buttons to push?"

"No. Wanted to be with you, that's all. Wanted to ask you something."

"Sure, ask away."

"I don't think Mister John believes in Mister God, do you Fynn?"

"Not sure," I said, "but I don't think he does."

"Oh."

I did try to tell her that not everybody in the world believed in Mister God, and that many people believed in something altogether different. That was difficult to explain and she did not believe me anyhow. For a little while she walked around the cases with me, looking at the various models, trying to get inside them in her imagination.

It was not long before John reappeared. "Glad I found you here, Fynn. I want to show you the exhibit over there. The Bush Differential Analyser. A very interesting device, really most interesting. What it does is . . ."

But he never did get around to telling us about it, and Anna wasn't much interested whatever it might do. There were questions she wanted to ask John and that was what she was going to do. I don't suppose that anybody had faced her questions so directly. She just hit him with them: "Mister John, why don't you believe in Mister God then? Why don't you?"

It wasn't often that John was lost for words, but he was on this occasion. He had to sit on a nearby seat. "Sit next to me, little one, and I'll try to tell you."

I wasn't certain how this was going to turn out at all. I wanted to be near her to give her support if she needed it. She had never heard him on the subject before and it was quite possible she might need a hand. I had quite forgotten the look she had given old Tyrannosaurus Rex.

I had never heard John be so gentle in all the years I had known him. He tried to explain so very simply that he couldn't possibly believe that it was all made in the way the Bible said. She listened without saying a word. He ended with, "so you see, little one, why I can't believe it. I'm sorry, but I can't."

For a long time nobody said a word. Anna, with her head hung down, was busy studying the floor. I hoped she had not been too hurt by what John had said and, from the looks he was giving me, it was obvious that he regretted the need for his words, but for John, the "truth" was all-important, no matter what the consequences. So there we sat, not knowing what to say. As she raised her head I did notice that little smile that she reserved for her "I haven't finished yet" times, so there was a lot more to come.

"How many pages in the Bible, Mister John? How many pages?"

"Pages?" he said. "Pages. I'm really not at all sure, but I suppose it must be around two thousand or more. Why do you ask?"

"How many pages when Mister God made the world, then? When he made it all."

"Not many. I don't think it was more than five, if that."

"That's like them skeleton things, ain't it Fynn? It don't matter do it?"

Since I didn't know what would come next, and the fact that I was always being dragged into this sort of thing, there was nothing much I could say.

"It's all them other pages, Mister John. It's all in them."

"What is, my little maid? What's in those pages?"

With a kind of "I told you so" flourish, she ended up with: "All the meat to put on them bones, them skeletons."

All that John could manage was, "I see. I must remember that." John was somewhat put out to have all his facts and figures so easily dismissed with the words "no meat," but she wasn't talking about the flesh of those long-dead beasties. It was something else entirely. I hoped she wasn't going to start on that . . . I had had that one for weeks.

So far as Anna was concerned, her "no meat" referred to all those equations and formulae and things that John had taught me, and that I so loved messing about with. She had told me quite clearly and simply that all that kind of stuff was just a lot of old bones, skeletons. Not that she had anything against them at all, but the really important thing to do was to put meat on them. She did manage to tell him: "They ain't got no outside, Mister John," and after a moment, "no insides, too." You've got to admit that it's difficult to get very excited about something that has got no outsides or insides.

For a few weeks the kids' conversation had been all about the coming bonfire night and how many fireworks they might have. It was to take place on Moonground, that place that the adults insisted on calling "the dump." For the kids, it was a place of imagination and invention, a place where the normal rules were changed to who-knows-what — like all scrap heaps, it was simply a jumble of the junk of living. There were times when I thought of it as a place where the ordinary rules had failed. It had been called Moon-ground for as long as I could remember. The adults knew it as a place to be avoided, a dangerous place, an eyesore, a place which somebody really ought to do something about! I had been trying to persuade John and his sister to come to see the kids and Moon-ground, and eventually it was agreed that we would all meet at seven o'clock on Bonfire Night. I always found it a slightly odd experience, standing in the middle of Moon-ground, for not too far away we could see the tower of our parish church where the Rev. Castle talked about another land where the rules were different, and where everything was very much better, because Jesus had stood the old rules on their head. Moonground was such a place, where the rules were both different and better. That was why grown ups did not like it. They felt uneasy because they did not know the rules, and they could not play with Mister God. They couldn't see it with different eyes.

"People see it with the same eyes," Anna had told me. "You've gotta see Moonground with different eyes."

I simply hadn't got the heart to tell her how difficult that was for most people. So I shut up.

So it was that Danny, Nob and I spent many

hours struggling to collect whatever was burnable and making a reasonable bonfire, whilst the kids were busy scrounging pennies: "Spare a penny for the guy, Mister."

Some of the older boys were busy making hand-warmers. A well-made hand-warmer was important for the coming winter months. Any person with a safe and well-made hand-warmer was always the centre of a huddle of kids. Some liked a large size cocoa tin with air holes punctured at the bottom and a lid that could be securely closed. This, fixed to about two feet of wire and a wooden handle, and you were ready to go. Once the paper, wood and coal in it were lit, a few energetic swings and twirls made it ready to warm the coldest of hands, and whoever had one was "Tops."

Come the appointed hour we all gathered at the end of the street, the older boys carrying large biscuit tins full of fireworks, and four or five swinging hand-warmers, like incense, as if they were in church. As we were going to Moonground along the Canal, Sally had decided we ought to take a few paraffin lamps to light our way along the towpath.

"Couldn't get no spuds, Fynn," yelled Heck. "Mum didn't have no money."

"It doesn't matter," I said. "We'll get some at the coffee stall."

"Got a bag of 'stickjaw'," chipped in Bunty.

"Good thing, too," said another. "It might stop you talking for a little while."

"Oh, you're a rotten thing, you, you're rotten!"

"Anybody got anything else?" I asked.

"A bag of peanuts . . ."

"I got some toasted coconut squares," said another.

We were slowly collecting a small feast.

"Ain't you got nothing, Fynn?" asked Kath.

"Sure I have," I replied. "Got some bars of chocolate and a bag of wine gums."

"You got anything, Mill?" asked Nipper.

"Sure have," replied Millie. "It's for grown ups like me, not for kids like you lot."

"I'm grown up," cried Kath. "Ain't I growed up? Give us a look, Mill. What you got in the bag? Eh?"

"Just you keep your nose to yourself. Keep your nose out of my bag."

"Betcha it's booze, ain't it, Mill?"

"Betcha a million pounds it's whisky . . . I betcha."

"What's it taste like, Mill?"

"Gi's a taste!"

"Nope," laughed Millie. "Nothing doing. It's just for me and Sally. You've gotta keep the damp and cold out when you're as old as me."

"How old's our Millie, Fynn?" asked Anna.

"Search me, Tich. I've got no idea."

"I'n she old like wot she said?"

"Betcha she's fifty," chimed in Heck.

"Can't be," cried another. "Betcha she's not older than thirty-five, ain't you, Mill?"

"Hold it you lot," complained Millie. "You'll have me in a wheel chair if you lot go on like that. If you really want to know, I'll be twenty on Christmas Eve."

"That's rotten, that is, ain't it?" said Rose. "You get one present and not two, do you?"

"Gonna have a party, Mill? Can I come?"

". . . and me?"

The continuous chatter of the kids spilled into the cold night air, the mist rising from the Canal and the breath of all the excited kids wove patterns in the light of the lamps, like newly formed ghosts. The shapes, unable to sustain themselves, disappeared. As we approached the bridge to cross the Canal we could see our bonfire on the other side. A rocket hurled itself into the sky, trailing its lace-tail of sparks.

As we approached the fence which we would all have to wriggle through by the light of the fire, I could see John's car parked at the far end of Moonground. I had forgotten that entirely, and wondered how he had managed to get it in. No doubt Danny or Sam had figured out some way of doing it. The early ones had certainly made a good bonfire. As we searched for an easy way in, we were confronted by PC Laithwaite on the other side of the fence.

"This way," he said, "and mind how you go. Glad to see you're all sensible this year. None of your dangerous backyard fires like last year. It's about time you older ones started to use your loaf," he remarked, directing that one at me. "There's hope for you yet. Come in and enjoy yourselves and mind you make sure the fire is well and truly out before you leave. I see young Fynn is with you. Oh, how are you Millie? Nice to see you get a night off then."

"I wouldn't miss this little shindig for all the tea in China," replied Millie.

"Sadie and Sally's here too."

"Do you good," he replied. "Off with you and have a nice time!"

Arabella came to meet us as we wandered towards the fire. "I've brought some baked potatoes with me," she said, "and enough sausages to feed an army. Hope I've done enough," she remarked, looking around at the kids. "You'll only need to warm them up."

Anna and I went over to greet John.

"You came, Mister John. That's nice."

Danny had made John comfortable on the rear seat we had taken out of an old wreck of a car a few days ago.

"Hello, little Anna," replied John. "Come and sit beside me."

She did more than that, much to his surprise, for she gave him a hug and a kiss, as did Millie and, encouraged by this display of affection, the other kids decided it was about time they joined in too. What with the red glow of the fire and the glow of his own pleasure, he looked happier than I had ever known him to be.

It was when Millie, the gentle tart from the backstreets, handed him a double whisky, that he nearly came apart at the seams.

"Have a tot, Prof.," she said, "keeps the cold outta yer bones."

For a moment or two he was quite undecided what to do, but finally he said, "Will you come and sit the other side of me, Miss Millie?"

"Sure thing, Prof.," she said. "I'd luv to," and plopped down with a flurry of skirts and legs. Poor old John. It must have been many years ago, if at all, that he had met anyone like Millie and he shifted a bit to make more room for her; but he had not reckoned with Millie! For she tucked an arm through his with "Us old 'uns gotta keep each other warm, ain't we Prof.?" Dear Millie. No matter how she earned her living, there was an innocence about her that it was impossible to miss. John smiled and relaxed, and there they sat, the loving pair, the earnest Professor and the questioning Anna.

Suddenly the night sky was afire with multi-coloured lights and showers of brilliant sparks.

"Watch this one," warned Danny as an extra large rocket climbed rapidly skyward and blossomed into a shower of coloured stars.

As the sparks slowly faded, Millie said, "It's good to know the stars are still there when all the fuss is over, ain't it, Prof.?"

He nodded, and turning to Anna, he asked, "Are you enjoying it?"

"Yes," she replied, ". . . but . . ."

"But what?"

"Mister John, what happens when the stars go out? What happens then?"

After the fireworks had finished and the fire had died down to a large mound of glowing embers, Danny and Sam went off to the pub for some bottles of pop and such stuff for the kids. We all sat around on old oil drums, packing cases or whatever could be found, reheating our baked potatoes and sausages. The kids began to sing. It amused me that they knew the words of the . . . well . . . naughty songs far better than the other ones. Soon Moonground faded into strange odd lumps, lit only by a few gas lamps from the street nearby, and the stars took on that strange nearness of a cold frosty night. John had been asked more questions in the last two hours than perhaps he had had for the last two years.

"Mister John, why are some of the sparks of them fireworks green and some of 'em blue?" and "What makes rockets go up? What, Mister John?"

By this time Anna was lying almost full length, staring up into the stars with that silence which so often heralds an outburst of questions. I edged towards her, expecting at any moment to be asked impossible questions. But I was to be spared it this night, for her questions were aimed at John.

"Mister John," she asked, "how many stars up there?"

"I think," he said after a moment's thought, "there are about three thousand stars that you can see and many, many more that you can't see even with a telescope."

She tucked that bit of information away somewhere as she silently rehearsed the next bit.

"Mister John," she said, pointing upwards, "if you join a line from that star to that star and then to that one, and then to . . ." she rattled off more stars. "If all them stars were joined up by little lines," John was giving nods of his head.

"Yes," he said, "I've got that."

"What then?"

John was preparing to give some astronomical explanation.

"Then it makes my face, don't it," she asked everybody in general.

I think John's lower jaw dropped an inch or two and I must say I reckon I had joined up a few stars the wrong way round, because I couldn't see it.

"Why ain't it *my* face?" exclaimed Bombom.

"It is too. It is your face too, Bombom," replied Anna. "It's everybody's face if you do it proper, ain't it, Mister John?"

Poor old John, he could do nothing more than nod his head! She hadn't finished yet.

"How many different faces in all them stars, Mister John? Eh?"

It wasn't the kind of question that John wanted to be exact with.

"So many," he said finally, "so many you couldn't count them."

"More than everybody in the world?" she went on.

He could do no more than nod silently. We were all silent as we looked for our faces in the stars.

"You wouldn't get my old man up there," giggled Heck.

"Why not, Heck?" I asked.

"He's so bloody ugly, Fynn," laughed Heck. "He'd frighten the life outta everybody. But he's a good 'un, a good 'un for sure!"

Sam had gone across to John's car, to get it onto the road. A few of us carried the old blanket and hamper that Arabella had brought with the various goodies in.

"Did you like it, Mister John? Good, wasn't it? That blooming big rocket, betcha it nearly went up to the Moon, betcha it did.

Didn't it, Mister John?"

"A long way," smiled John. "It certainly went up a long way."

I was glad that he didn't launch into some mathematical calculation in order to give some more accurate estimation of just how high it had reached. He shook his head and, to my complete surprise, said, "Perhaps it did go up as high as the moon."

"Told you so . . . told you, didn't I?"

Something had made him see the magic of this night and not simply the facts. As we walked, John put his hand on my shoulder.

"You must be tired, John," I said. "Can I do anything?"

"I'm not really all that tired," he replied, "more . . . well, more thoughtful."

"What about?" I asked.

"Looking back."

"Oh!"

"Did I? It's too long. I can no longer remember. Did I?"

"Did you what?" I asked.

He gave a long, long sigh. "Did I ask so many questions when I was that age? I can no longer remember that far back." He paused for a moment. "Where does the magic go to, I wonder? Where? Where?"

I didn't answer that one, for in the first place, this wasn't the moment, and in the second place, I didn't know the answer.

They were just about to drive off.

"Bring her to see me. Bring her often . . . little Anna!"

I promised I would.

From somebody or from somewhere Anna had very early on picked up the idea that answers came first and questions came later. This wasn't the way I had been taught and it certainly would not do for Old John. Mum had perfected this way of living for a long time, so when Anna and Mum came together, they were a well matched pair! It was a little tough on me, for I never really knew if I was coming or going, and, more often than not I found myself trying to go both ways at once. That can be a little painful at times.

At times I did complain that Answers really ought to come after the Questions, but I never did make much headway with this approach. I was smiled at. Being smiled at in that particular way could be very tough to take. It could reduce me in size immediately.

"There is mess in every order," Mum said, "and an order in every mess, but whatever order you may find or whatever mess you make, it's yours — nobody else's!"

It was not unusual for some people to liken Anna to something or somebody that they understood. "She's like a jackdaw or a magpie, she picks up these things." I did it myself, I likened her to an angel. Not that I knew all that much about angels, I can't remember if I've ever met one or not, but I was a bit surprised when John likened her to a rifle. That stumped me completely!

"Have you ever fired a rifle, Fynn?"

"Nothing bigger than a peashooter or a popgun. Why do you ask?"

"She reminds me of one."

"A bomb I could understand, I feel as if I've been blown up at times!" I replied, "but a rifle, never."

I don't think he liked what he had said. He was struggling for words.

"Hell! There are times when she appears to have a foresight and a backsight. Don't be so dense, young Fynn. You sure know what I'm driving at."

"You've lost me, John, give with the explanation."

"I suppose what I am trying to say is that you align with the foresight and adjust with the backsight."

"Sounds all right to me," I said, "but what's to do with it?"

"Not much, I suppose, except she knows exactly what she's aiming for. I wish I could say the same for myself. She causes me to have the strangest thoughts. Idiot thoughts. Things that I know can't be true, but they're there."

Now I was in a muddle. He seemed to be thinking like Anna and I said so.

"Perhaps you're right, Fynn, perhaps so.

"Does she ever give you the feeling that she is . . ."

"Is what?"

"A detached part of your own memory? She does me. I'm losing my grip on things."

"Not you, John. Not you!"

"Often she reminds me of my own child-hood, my own memories, my own muddles."

"Muddles I can understand," I said. "She often stands me on my head."

"Now you're laughing at me. You're not to! I don't like it one bit."

"Sorry, John, but you did it often enough to me."

"I know," he said, "but that was different. I was a lot older than you and it was, after all, my duty to teach and yours to learn. She can give me a positive mental itch at times, and I just don't know how to scratch it. Mental indigestion, I suppose, but Fynn . . ."

"Yes?"

"There are times when I think she may be right, not in the bigger things, you under-stand, but in the smaller things. If only she could explain herself accurately it would help."

"It would help me too," I laughed, "if you could tell me what you're on about. I'm lost."

"Has she," he asked, "assaulted you with her very, very, very world?"

"Oh that one," I said, "I got that one in the middle of the night weeks ago! The very, very, very small and the very, very, very large. Something she picked up somewhere. Perhaps somebody wrote it down for her, or maybe one of my books . . ."

"That I can understand, but where did she get the idea that the rules were different? Did she work it out or did somebody tell her? She's right, you know."

"That puzzles me far less than the fact that she looked up the word 'very' in the dictionary. I did many, many years ago. It's not a word I use often. Do you know the meaning of the word?"

"Never given it a thought. I just use it."

"Only that it means real or true, and that's what I'm not at all sure about."

John was now spending as much time with the kids at our home as I spent at Random Cottage. It was strange to see this retired teacher sitting on an old crate or the old car seat which was always called "Mister John's place." In no time at all he was perfectly at ease with Millie and her pals at the top of the street. No longer did he judge them or criticize them. Certainly he was saddened by the fact that they had chosen that way of making money because they could see no other way of helping their families out. He put it correctly, when he said to me, "You're very lucky to have such good friends."

And I was so lucky.

I'm fairly sure that I had never heard Anna use the word "preface" in any of her chatterings, but she certainly understood that the beginning part of a book told you what the book was going to be all about, and that was just the skeleton, wasn't it? It was the rest of the book, "the meat," that helped you to understand it all. So when John told her that he couldn't believe in Mister God because he just couldn't believe the beginning, she wasn't all that surprised. Just saddened. She had seen shelves and shelves of books in his study, so he must know that the beginning bit was only the skeleton, mustn't he? He did agree with her when she explained it to him, but it didn't help him all that much. It was funny how grown-up people did that kind of thing. They just didn't bother with all the nice meaty bits, but they were always ready to fight each other about the skeletons. Like the Rev. Castle. He always talked about Mister God as if he was like a very strict Head Master with a cane in his hand, just waiting to punish everybody. It was no wonder his sermons were so often punctuated by her overloud "Pooh!" So far as Anna was concerned, Mister God was definitely and positively cuddly. It makes a difference if you start off that way.

"It isn't that I think she's right. It's what she says, young Fynn. Nothing like that at all, but then . . ."

"I know what you mean, John. It's always 'but then' with her!"

"She puts so many different things together in one idea that, to me, it's just a muddle."

"To me, too. I never know for certain if I'm up or down."

"But then she always wriggles out of her muddle somehow."

"It's the way she has of saying things."

"I find myself waiting for the next bit. I'm surprised to find I'm holding my breath and I haven't done that for many years."

When talking about Anna, I so often find I run out of words. I don't know what to say next. I did manage to say: "She just sees things in a different way, that's all John."

"Maybe, maybe, except that she has the knack of making things look beautiful. Even her own complicated muddles. She puzzles me, Fynn, and I don't mind saying it. The most I would like to say about the little maid is that she makes me stop and think again. Does she ever write stories, Fynn?"

"Yes, quite often."

"Perhaps she might write some for me sometime?"

"Why don't you ask her yourself? Better still, why don't you ask her to tell you one of them."

"Perhaps I will."

That winter didn't treat John kindly. On too many occasions he had to stay in his room with some bug or other, which meant our visits were far less frequent and much shorter than usual. But on those occasions when we did manage to have a little chat, he appeared to be very much more thoughtful. His decisive, cold edge was no longer there. He seemed far more inclined to listen, rather than to launch into some complex lesson as to the nature of things. I'm really not certain how he would have taken comment on his change. "He's more cuddly," Anna had said.

I'm not certain that I would have used those words but change there certainly was. He no longer had that unshakeable certainty. He was more given to listen to other views and, most curious to me, he asked questions, which was something I rarely heard him do. On those occasions that I did manage to get a question in, the answer was often, "I'm not sure, Fynn," or, "I don't know." On a number of occasions when we had been talking about one thing or another, he had turned away from me and said to Anna, "What do you think, my little one?" I had the distinct feeling that he was wanting to capture some of Anna's fire or some of her excitement of the nature of things. Maybe I was just letting my imagination run loose, but it certainly seemed that way to me. I was beginning to feel that it was her that he really wanted to talk to, not me. For in many ways we were far too much alike for me to be of any help to him at all. My main contribution in this threesome was as a sort of interpreter.

For much of the time I don't think they were all that aware that I was even there. Old John was even beginning to giggle. Not the kind of giggle you did behind a raised hand, but a full-blooded giggle of joy. At the start of these giggles, he had often apologized, but now he would take her by the hand and let go. It was good to see the pair of them laughing so happily together. There were secrets between them that I was unable to share. For they divined in each other something that I was unable to reach. In spite of all their laughter, though, I felt that beneath it all John was having a pretty rough time. He was wrestling with something and I didn't know what it was, and neither John nor Anna was prepared to tell me. Not only was I often asked to go and do something else, things which so far as I could see were completely unnecessary, but I was also firmly told to take my time about it!

"Go and get some doughnuts at the shop, Fynn. I'm sure Anna would like a doughnut or two for her tea. I certainly would." I was completely unable to tell him that there was a bag of doughnuts in a tin in the kitchen. So off I went and left them to it. I didn't really mind all that much doing these little things, but I was taken aback when, after a bit of shopping and after I had put the tea tray down in the drawing room, he turned to me and said, "Doughnuts, Fynn? You should know by now that I never eat the things. Isn't there a jam tart in the kitchen or just a plain bun or something?"

I very nearly told him that not only were there jam tarts, there were plain buns, fruit cake and at least six more doughnuts in the kitchen, but I didn't. It didn't really seem worth it!

It wasn't that Mum was so much better than anybody else that made her so different. She wasn't beyond the odd cuss word now and again, and her temper on those few occasions when she lost it was really something to see. That was the time to duck! No, it was altogether something different — simpler.

In her view, the reason why this old world got itself in such a tangle wasn't because people either did or didn't believe that there was a God. It was quite simply the fact that everybody wanted to do more than God. As she put it, "Nobody ever told you that you've got to do more than God, did they?" I had never heard it said and it certainly wasn't that Mum didn't work hard, she did. But she always kept time for herself, time when she just liked being with all those crazy things that went with just being. She could simply turn off. Anna could do it with ease. Turning off came naturally to her, but with me it was hard work. It took me a long time to learn that. As Mum put it, how could you read a book if there were no spaces between the words? and music would sound like I don't know what without its own intervals!

The New Year had arrived for me almost unnoticed, except for the fact that we were all going to be a year older. Anna was fast growing up, both in her size and her pursuit of beauty. I had recently bought myself a tandem. It would be much safer to make our journeys on that than to have her perched on my handle-bars, where her continuous wriggling about was a bit of a hazard, to say the least. That year Anna was going to be seven so we decided that we would go off to see John and show him our almost new tandem. It hadn't taken much to alter the rear seat and the handle-bars, and we were all set for off. I don't think she had really noticed the pedals and that they were there in order to help the thing along! I really didn't mind at all, doing all the pedalling, and she found it easier to look at things as we went along much better than when wriggling around on the handle-bars.

John gave it a really close inspection as he walked around it.

"You may find this difficult to believe, young Fynn," he said, "but I was once very good on one of these contraptions. Once the weather gets a lot warmer you must let me use it for a little ride."

"I'll steer it, Mister John," said Anna.

"I think," he replied a little doubtfully, "we had better wait until you are a bit older."

"I'm nearly seven," she replied. "That's old."

"Seven!" he said. "That's old is it? Well, well, well. I'm nearly . . ." He started to give his age and then thought better of it. He merely said, "That makes me very old, then."

I went into the house with John for a pint of refreshment, leaving Anna to wander around in the garden. We both raised our tankards and wished each other a "Happy New Year" and then he said, "That little one out there has made me realize something I really ought to have known. It's an error that I really can't account for."

"What's that, John?" I asked, quite uncertain as to what this terrible error might be.

He chuckled deep in his throat before he answered. "I suppose I had assumed that the mind was a sort of array of little cupboards, each one clearly marked with its particular subject." He ticked off a number on his fingers — "Mathematics, English, Science, Geography, and . . . maybe Religion too."

I didn't think he wanted any answer to that one, so I just waited for him to continue. "You can see my point, young Fynn, can't you?"

I shook my head.

"Well, maybe not, but I'll tell you this. After listening to little Miss Chatterbox," he said pointing to the window, "I've begun to think that you can't organize your mind in the same way you can order your books. It just doesn't work that way."

I did know the next question to ask, but I never got the chance.

"No, Fynn," he continued, "whatever goes in the mind must, I suppose, be, to some degree, altered by what is already there."

"Sounds all right to me. I'll go for that."

"This attitude of wonder and excitement that Anna has is something that I think I've never possessed. It makes a difference, you know, Fynn. It prevents you keeping everything apart. I won't say that I think she's always right in what she says, but I do admit that I was wrong in dismissing it all too easily. What a mix up. It is all a mix up, to be sure, Fynn. Like everybody else I have not been without hope, but I need to be convinced. Not that the little maid has convinced me, but it's the silly little things that she says that make me doubt my own doubt. A few days ago I asked her how did she know that Mister God was true and that he was really there. She simply said she could feel him because he is warmer than me. 'That's why, if Mister God wasn't different, I wouldn't know, would I?'

"I did ask her about Satan. 'Old Nick is colder,' she had said. You know, Fynn, the way she has of putting things does make sense. I suppose my mistake has been that I have never really put it to the test. Perhaps I ought not to quiz her too vigorously, Fynn, but she does have an answer to all my questions. Not that I understand her answers!

"I asked her, 'Where do I find Mister God?' Her answer didn't give me any comfort at all! Her answer to that little question was 'in people's puzzles.' What do you make of that one, Fynn? I suppose she could be right. There I go again, Fynn, I do get too technical at times, but I have no other way. It's difficult for me to think about something that is not open to inspection. All you are left with is to say what Mister God is like, and the little maid can be quite convincing there. All her dratted circles and colours make a nice point. I've always found that the usual talk about God leaves God as a remote and abstract thing, not the warmth that Anna talks about. I suppose if you are able to involve something in everything and that everything's in that something, that has to be the answer to Mister God. She seems to be able to do that with such ease and I must say, I like it. Sorry to sound so clinical, Fynn, that's the way I am, I'm no expert. On the other way, I need a great deal of practice. She always reminds me of an insurance company, if you see what I mean."

The remark was beyond me.

"It's the ignorance of the one thing that can, if you go about it in the right way, lead to knowledge of the many things. There I go again, but I do find her way most compelling."

John did have a rough time with Anna, with what he called the "invisible stings of childhood" and his wish to see things with other eyes.

One thing was certain. He had changed a great deal.

Tea didn't take long that afternoon. All she really wanted was to get into the garden.

"Well, well, well, what caused that little eruption?"

"I don't think anything caused it," I said. "It's just one of those things that happen now and again. I think I need something stronger than tea. A pint might be better, or maybe even two."

"It might at that, Fynn, it might at that. It was as well I retired when I did. I was really getting too old for it. The thought of the brat every day of my life was . . . well . . . too much. No, not that, Fynn, let's say very rich. She never leaves you with nothing to think of, does she?"

"That's for sure. How do you like the thought

of sticking the universe in your ear, John?"

"Not a pleasant thought, to be sure, but I see no way of getting out of the dilemma. Perhaps we really are the wrong size after all. I must give it some serious thought."

"While you are thinking, John, spare a moment to think about my problem too. How the devil do you talk to angels?"

"Not talk, Fynn. Do sums. There's a difference. Perhaps not much, but there must be one."

We did have another pint before we left and had it not been for my passenger there might have been one more.

"Good luck with the angels, Fynn!" he said as we left. "I have great faith in you and know that you'll manage something to her satisfaction."

"Nuts!" I said and we were off.

"Growing up," John said to me one evening over a pint of beer, "Growing up — what the devil does that mean?"

"Don't ask me. If you don't know by now I don't know who does."

"Gently, gently, my young Fynn. Please don't rub it in. It must have something to do with understanding, I suppose. Otherwise, what else?"

"Perhaps it ought to, but it doesn't always

turn out that way, does it?"

"Conformity to other people's ideas, that's what it is. Conformity!"

"Oh! What brought that on?"

"The little maid. I have been thinking a lot about her recently. I still don't understand her. Perhaps I never will."

"Perhaps we aren't meant to," I replied.

"Meant, Fynn, meant! Don't give me any more of that gush. Nobody means us to be anything except us and none of us are very good at that. Conformity is just too much to pay for the pleasures of living. I know that I'm much older than you, young Fynn, and I just don't like it. Not one bit. The little one has got something that I haven't got and it's puzzled me for weeks. I know what it is. It's something I lost too many years ago. Something I should have guarded with my life. I never realized that until a few weeks ago. Conformity robbed me of it and I never noticed until now."

"What is it, John? What did you lose?"

"A vision. Just that I had one once, but not now. Sometimes little Anna's chatter reminds me of it, but it's not there any longer, I'm afraid."

"A vision, John? Don't we all have them?"

"I'm sure we do, but conformity knocks it out of us and then it's too late."

"Not with you, John. Not certain what you're saying. What do you mean?"

"Exactly what you have said. You don't know what I mean. The little one would never make that mistake, she would know."

"That's beyond me, John. You just confuse me and that's not like you!"

He chuckled. "Haven't you ever noticed, Fynn, that a vision, like love, has its own language that you can never find in a dictionary. The little one knows that so she has to invent a way of words that is different. I hear what she says well enough and I listen well enough. Perhaps I hear it too well and I correct what I hear, but there are so many times when I just don't listen. Perhaps that's the difficulty of growing older, hearing — but not listening. Blasted kids," he grinned, "they listen, but so seldom hear! Remind me again of that saying that your mother so often uses."

"What one is that John? She uses so many!"

"The one about stopping."

"Oh, the one about if you haven't stopped in the course of the day then you just haven't done anything worthwhile. Is that the one?"

"Yes, that's the one. It's crazy, just plain stupid, until you stop and listen and then it makes sense."

"That's what we call 'doughnut speech' at home."

"Who called it that name?" he asked.

"Anna of course, who else?"

"That's exactly the point I'm driving at. With a vision, you are forced to invent words. I had forgotten that that's why you have to listen so hard. The straight and narrow sounds all right, but if you're not careful, all you learn are the tricks of the trade and nothing else. I used to think at one time that everything could be written into a book, but now I'm not sure. Books might contain what you need to know, but where, oh where, do you find what you want to know? I'm very tired of tricks, Fynn, and I envy you more than I can say."

"Why do you say that, John?"

"Both your mother and the little maid have a vision. It might make life very difficult for you, but don't lose it. There sure must be more than words to it all, Fynn, don't you think so? There are times when I am of the opinion that they are more of a hindrance than a help. What is there other than words? There's nothing else to use."

"I know Anna's answer to that, John," I replied. "Beauty."

"She might have something there at that,

but we still need words, for how else can we share beauty?"

"You'd better ask Mum about that. She reckons that when you come face to face with beauty there is nothing else to do except remain silent."

"Your mother and the little maid have an answer for everything. It is just possible it's right, but it's so difficult to remain silent you know, young Fynn. You may think that I am against the Bible entirely. I'm not. I do admit to being puzzled about the first and the last chapters of the Bible, but everything else I understand up to a certain point. It puzzled me when I was a child and it still does now. Fynn, answer me one question and then I'll be satisfied. Who was God talking to in the first chapter of Genesis?"

"Nobody, as far as I know," I said.

"I'm glad you don't know either. It always puzzled me when God says 'Let us make man in our own image.' Who was this 'us' He was talking to? That's where I must have lost my vision. I think it's puzzled me all my life. It was very early in my life I resolved to dispel the mystery of it and preserve the wonder. I don't think I've made a good job of that. It depresses me, but then I am encouraged to read the lines 'and God saw that it was good.' Perhaps it means beautiful. Do you think so, Fynn?"

"Could be, John, could be. I don't really know."

"I'm always so happy when you bring the little maid to see me, you must do it more often. No, no Fynn, don't say it is because I'm old and she is so young. It's not that at all. Nor do I understand her chattering, but every once in a while she uncovers a beauty for me that I had lost. Do you understand what I'm saying, Fynn?"

"I think so," I replied.

"The nerve of her! The last time you were here she told me I was wrong."

"How did that come about?" I asked him.

"I happened to say that she was magic."

"So?"

"Her answer was so hard to believe that I thought for a moment that she was regarding herself too highly, much too highly, but I was wrong."

"Come on John, let's have it. What did she say?"

" 'No Mister John,' she said, 'I'm not magic, I'm a miracle!' What do you make of that?"

"Just being her normal self, I suppose."

"No, you're making the same mistake as I did. 'Miracles,' she told me, 'was when you said sorry to Mister God and he took you back to find what you had lost.' I'm not at all certain about saying sorry to Mister God, but there is a lot of truth in taking you back to find what you have lost, so who knows, maybe she is a sort of miracle. So, Fynn, bring her as often as you can."

There was no doubt about it. John had changed a lot since I had first met him. He was certainly a lot mellower, although with me he could still be tough and still the same old stringy John that I had first met. With Anna he was much gentler, which was strange,

231

because it was me he ought to have been gentle with. He just didn't know how tough Anna really was! Like so many people who spent much time with Anna, they so often got it wrong. Sure she was sweet, sure she was all the things that you might drool over in a child, but when, like me, you could be woken up at any time of night to talk about "them things" you began to see her in a different light. At three o'clock in the morning, to be faced with the question, "Fynn, them things you was talking about yesterday — what does it do?" or maybe, "What does it mean?" She never did realize that at that time in the morning I had enough problems trying to figure out what I was, let alone trying to explain what "them things" were, particularly when "them things" could be almost anything from a rice pudding to a volcano. I didn't see her as sweet at these times, but I didn't really mind. In fact, once I got over the shock of having my eyes opened, I really enjoyed it.

It was often in the middle of the night that things really happened. To wake up to her "Fynn, Fynn . . . the Vicar!"

"Eh! What? What about the Vicar. What's he been up to?"

"Why does he have to protect Mister God so much and make people frightened?"

"No idea, Tich."

"Why does he protect Mister God so much and attack people?"

"I've got no idea."

"Why does he do it then?"

"Dunno."

That wasn't my idea of a good night's sleep, but that was the way I got used to my nights, and this was one of the things about her that very few people knew, and as for her prayers that I heard every night, I often wondered what the Rev. Castle might say on that subject!

"Hello, Mister God. This is Anna talking," which was a nice way to start. There were also times when it seemed to me that it was her way of letting Mister God know who he was talking to. Her next words might easily begin, "Now look, Mister God . . ." or "Look here, Mister God . . ." She could just as easily give him a good scolding or tell him how wonderful everything was. I reckon you had to be pretty sure of Mister God to start off with "Now look, Mister God, you mustn't blame him or . . ." Anna was certainly sure about Mister God. So sure that the occasional ticking off was quite all right. It was at these moments when the sweetness that other people saw in her could turn her into something tougher than anybody realized. When John had spoken to me of Mum's and Anna's vision, he made me a little itchy. Visions were something I knew very little about. So far as I was aware, we were a little short of visions, visitations, voices and such like down our street. Everybody was far too busy doing lots of things with so very little to expect such wonderful happenings. When John had told me just how much he enjoyed being with her and listening to her chatter, he then said, "She probably is the complete eclectic." He made it sound as if she had got the measles or the plague or something like that. That was a new one to me. I had to look it up in the dictionary. "Eclectic" meant picking up those things that please her most, but what was wrong with that? It was true she picked up things, she picked other people's minds or other people's ideas, whatever pleased her. What John didn't realize then was that that was the easy bit. What she was then doing was re-arranging the bits she picked up or the bits that pleased her and, in due time, she would present this bouquet to Mister God. Not just a bunch, but a proper bouquet, one of the best arrangements possible. That's where she was a toughy. That took time. Sometimes what she wanted was hard to find.

On the day of the Sunday School outing, that once a year scramble for the kids, I was unable to go along with them. I had to work a few hours' overtime that Saturday morning. I did manage to get all the kids to the appointed place in time and we waited for the char-a-banc to arrive.

"Sorry you can't come, Fynn," said Millie, "but we've got enough of us to look after this lot."

After work I decided to spend a few hours with John. I did like talking to him and he was glad to see me when I arrived.

"Glad to see you, young Fynn. By yourself?"

"Anna's off to the seaside with the kids from the Sunday School."

We talked about this and that, drank a few pints and munched a few sandwiches, but Anna crept back into our conversation.

"Fynn, I'm never really sure if she's teasing me or not."

"I know what you mean. It's not that what she says always makes sense, far from it. All the same, I know what you're going to say, John. You must not, or cannot, ignore it or dismiss it completely."

"That is exactly it! She so often mixes up her subject matter so completely that I am not always certain what she's up to."

"I've been there before," I said.

"Often, nevertheless, Fynn, in spite of

what you and I might call a muddle, she does paint a most captivating picture. One that I wouldn't miss for anything."

"Don't worry, John, she won't let you miss anything!"

"You know my views on religious matters?"

"I have heard, John. I have heard!"

"It's her attitude to her precious Mister God that puzzles me so much. Of course, Fynn, it's none of my business whether anybody believes in God. By all means, if that's what gives you comfort . . ."

"Not comfort, John," I managed to say. "That's easy. It's joy, and that's not easy."

"As I was about to say, Fynn, she seems to know her particular God so well that I can't . . ." he paused for a long moment, ". . . can't tell them apart! It's always struck me as strange, Fynn."

"What has?"

"The fact that the less you know anybody, the greater are the differences that you can recognize, and conversely, the more you know a person, the more you realize just how alike you are."

"That's an interesting thought, John. It makes me wonder, if Mister God realizes just how alike he is to Anna he might have a bit of fun for a change."

"If I was a church-going man, Fynn, I

might say you were being sacrilegious, but as I am not a church-goer, I merely say that you're being facetious. Did it ever occur to you to wonder why I singled you out all those years ago?"

"No, but I did often wonder why it was always me that ended up with so many beatings."

"Oh that! It never did you any harm. I singled you out, for, in many ways, you reminded me of myself when I was your age."

"In what way was that, John?"

"Cocksure! Just bloody cocksure! Perhaps we just grew up too fast. You know, Fynn, bearing in mind what I said a few moments ago, you are beginning to sound like Anna at times. What a terrifying prospect for you, young Fynn."

"How's that, John?"

"To have both me and Anna inside you at one and the same time! No wonder you get so muddled at times. No offence meant, Fynn, no offence. Don't worry! They seem to fit well enough. I'm happy."

We talked in that fashion for hours.

"Fynn, it would be nice if other people could see me as you and Anna do. Most people see me as a cantankerous old Grouch. I suppose I am. When are the children back from their outing?"

"They are due at the church at six o'clock."

"Ah," he said. "You can put your bicycle in the back of the car and I'll drive you there. I'd like to see the kids again."

So, at the proper time we ended up at the church and, after a short wait, the char-a-banc arrived. In no time at all John found himself in the middle of a tangle of kids.

"Hi, Fynn," said Millie. "I'm done to a frazzle. I'm worn out!"

"How'd it go, Mill?"

"Like clockwork, like clockwork. My bloody spring's busted."

Slowly the kids found their mums and left, and I walked over to John and Anna.

"Fynn," he said, "I have suggested to Anna that she might like to come to my birthday party next Saturday, if that is convenient to you, that is. She can bring a few of her friends too. Not too many, of course, I really could not face all that lot." So the time and place was arranged and he went.

I was completely unable to suggest to Anna any present that John might like to have. Not with the money that was available, that is. So far as I could see, there was nothing much he didn't have. I had to leave it to her.

That week was a frenzy of activity. Whatever it was that was going on I was not allowed to see. I often saw Millie and Anna sitting with their backs to the railway wall, busy doing something or other, and in the kitchen, things were hurriedly put away. I got many a secret smile from Millie and Anna, but that was as far as I got. I knew that Millie was coming to the party and Bombom, May and Bunty, and that was as far as I knew. And I was told that we were going by bus, so we could sit upstairs in the front. Of course, there was no other way to go, not when you were nearly seven, that is. So armed with the fare money that I had given her, we boarded the bus and in due time we arrived at Random Cottage, polished and all shined up. John didn't try to shy away from Mill's warm kiss or from the rest of the kisses from the kids. After all, this was a very special day. The sitting room was full of people drinking cocktails and eating "funny things on sticks."

"I know you, Millie, would like a large whisky, and a pint of my special for you, Fynn? And for the children, there's lemonade, ginger pop and that kind of thing. What would you like to eat?"

All the various bits and pieces on sticks, so easily and rapidly rechristened "horses doofers," they didn't want. What they did want was toast and dripping, the meaty jelly stuff at the bottom of the basin.

Anna tugged at my arm. "The present, Fynn, when?"

"Now," I said, "right now."

And so John was wished "Happy Birthday" and handed various packages and "stickjaw" toffees. It was a pity that Bunty's offering of a bag of hundreds and thousands burst on its way to the table. Arabella's squeal alerted the whole company to this disaster, but we soon sorted that one out, and I took the kids off to the kitchen to hunt for toast and dripping, and in no time at all they were happily munching away. Considering how house-proud Arabella was, plus the fact that dripping has a habit of dripping everywhere, I decided that the place for us was in the kitchen out of all possible danger. It was there that John found us.

"I hope you've all had enough. Come along with me and meet everybody. Look, Anna," he said, "I'm wearing my badge," and he displayed his large beadwork red heart. "And as for your picture of me, I think that is wonderful."

This was news to me. I hadn't seen the heart before, nor the picture. We followed John back to the sitting room.

"Have you had your toast and dripping?" asked a lady.

"Yes, fanks, Missis," said Bunty. "Wasn't

arf good, too. It lines yer belly a treat that do." They all laughed.

"And this," said John, taking Anna forward by the hand, "is the young lady who drew my likeness." The likeness was of a face constructed from numbers and surrounded by hearts.

"How very clever of you to think of such an original idea," said a lady.

"It's so like John. Nothing but numbers."

"All them hearts are him too," corrected Anna. John glowed at this and placed his new likeness on the centre of the mantelpiece.

The party went well and eventually all the other guests left, leaving us alone. As Bombom was mincing up and down with an empty cocktail glass: "How original of you, my dear!" John was standing in the doorway. He did manage to move out of sight before he burst into laughter.

I had been in John's garden for near on a couple of hours. Arabella wanted that patch of thistles, docks and nettles turned into the usual well-ordered flower bed. I had managed to get it near to what she wanted, but by now even my blisters were getting blisters. It was time I packed it in. I was careful to tidy myself up, and put on a different pair of shoes so that I didn't tread mud all over the house.

Anna and John were heads down, battling away over a game of draughts. John lifted his head and pointed across the room.

"Pour yourself a pint, Fynn. I can recommend the new brew, and you might just as well bring me one, too."

I was thankful to get the weight off my feet, and sank into a comfortable armchair. I managed one long drink and then it happened.

"It's like Mister God, ain't it, Mister John?"

John didn't answer.

"Ain't it like Mister God, Fynn?"

I didn't move. After all, since, according to Anna, almost everything was like Mister God in one way or another, it came as no surprise to me to learn that playing a game of draughts was like Mister God. I didn't know how it was, but it really didn't matter, for in due time we would be told. John wasn't at all used to this kind of thing and showed his impatience.

"Get on with it, it's your move."

"Fynn, if Mister John is Mister God and I'm me, this is where it starts."

John had been called many things before, but never ever had he been called "Mister God," and he didn't know which way to look.

He always found it difficult to pretend.

"Fynn, here! Look!"

There was little use in making a fuss, so I just got up and went.

"He's Mister God over there and I'm me here."

"Yeah, I know that."

I looked at John and raised my eyebrows.

"Fynn, don't you dare. Don't you dare say anything!"

I couldn't resist it. "He's Mister God and you're you, I've got that bit. What's next?" I said.

"Then I'm going that way to him and he's going this way to me."

"Uh, uh, that's the usual way it's done."

"So it is a bit like Mister God, ain't it, Fynn? It's got to be." She nodded her agreement with herself.

"Then what happens?" I asked.

She thought for a moment before she launched into the next bit.

"Fynn," she exclaimed with excitement, "if I get home to his side he's gotta turn me into a King, don't he?"

"What happens," I managed to ask, "if he gets to your side? How do you work that one out?"

"Well," she replied, "he can turn himself into anything he likes, can't he?"

Although this wasn't the kind of conversation John ever got himself involved in, he did manage to ask a question.

"Anna, my dear, what happens in the middle? After all, that is where the game is played."

"Course it is, I know that."

"Well?" I asked.

She looked at John and me as if we were some form of idiot.

"Well," she announced, "you gotta be careful then, don't you?"

"It's all really too simple when you know how, isn't it?"

"You finish off my game, Fynn. Must have a pee."

John looked at me and laughed. "How does she do it, Fynn, how?"

"Search me," I said. "I haven't found the answer yet."

"She seems to be able to wriggle out of the most complicated situations," he said.

"Well," I added, "there are times when she simply shifts it over to you. If you want to play you've got to be prepared for the changes."

It was about the middle of October. The days were beginning to get noticeably shorter. I was having a chinwag with Millie and Danny at the top of the street. The gaslamps were never all that bright, and I didn't notice Arabella until she was almost on top of us. She very nearly tumbled and certainly would have done so, had Danny not held her up.

"Fynn, can you come? John wants to see you, I think he might die. Fynn, do you think that you could bring Anna, too?"

"I'm not at all sure. How bad is he?"

"I think he's very bad. The doctor is with him now. Fynn, please ask Anna. She wouldn't be frightened, would she? Not with you."

"I'll go and ask Mum and Anna," I said. "Would you like to come down with me or would you rather stay here?"

Millie said: "You stay here with us, Arabella, and let Fynn sort it out at home. You hold on here and I'll pop across the road for a whisky. You look as if you could do with a lifter."

"How about getting you home after all this?" asked Danny. "I've got my motorbike around the corner and you're welcome to a ride if you like."

"It'll have to do, won't it?" she said.

I returned about this point with the news that Mum had said it was all right if Anna wanted to go. So Mum was already getting my tandem onto the street and Anna was putting on something warm. Danny went off to get his motorbike as Millie returned with the whisky and a stool for Arabella to sit on.

"Fynn," she said, "I think that we are going to lose him this time. He has had too many little attacks in the last few years, but this,

Fynn, this one is big and I don't really know what to do."

Mum turned up, pushing my tandem, along with Anna following behind. "Anything I can do?" she asked.

"Wish I knew what," I said, "I don't think so."

"If there is," said Mum as she turned to go, "give Mrs Bartlett a ring and I'll certainly do what I can. If you have to stop, that'll be all right. I know where you are, but do be careful on this dark night. Be careful and don't go along the Canal. Stick to the road. See you when I see you then. Take care."

I promised I would. A minute or two later the roar and rattle of Danny's bike heralded the fact that he was nearly with us.

"Sorry I was so long. I had to find a cushion for the pillion seat. Sorry about the noise, Arabella, but the old exhaust is getting a bit dicky, but it'll get us there all right. Oh, and keep your leg away from it, it does get a bit hot. I can't think of any other way of getting you home."

"This will do just fine."

"It'll have to, Fynn," he said. "I'll get off now, so we'll be waiting for you."

With one last adjustment of the exhaust they were off. It was a sober little group that listened to the fading roar of that engine. By this time there must have been twenty or so people huddled around that lamp post.

"Hope he's gonna be all right," said Bombom.

"He ain't gonna die, is he, Fynn?" asked May.

"Don't know, luv," I replied. "We'll just have to wait and see."

"He's a nice old geezer." This was from Nipper.

"How long it'll take you to get there?" asked Millie.

"Ten, maybe fifteen minutes," I replied. "Suppose we'd better get off then. You on, Tich?"

"I'm ready, Fynn."

"Hope it'll turn out all right, Fynn. Give him our love, if you can," said Millie.

I promised I would do that if I could.

"And, Fynn," she yelled as we moved off, "give us a ring if you need any help."

I wanted to speed along as quickly as I could, but with Anna on the back, I had to be extra careful. What with all the tramlines, the dimly lit streets and those damn cobble stones I just had to concentrate. My passenger was silent for the whole journey. I was not used to this lack of chatter, but in the circumstances it was a good thing. It allowed me to give my full attention to getting us there in one piece. About two hundred yards from Random Cottage, we met Danny pushing his motor bike on the homeward journey. I pulled into the side of the road, "Hi, Da. Trouble?"

"No. Thought I'd better push this old contraption away from the house before I start her up. She can make a bit of a racket at times. Wait a tick, Fynn, will you? I might need a bit of a push. There's somebody there, Fynn. There's a couple of cars in the drive. Don't know who. Maybe the doctor. Don't know. You're to go straight into the sitting room."

By then his motorbike was shattering the night air. It really was about time he got a new exhaust. I waited a few minutes until the sound of his engine faded into the distance. It was a matter of holding on to something familiar for a while longer.

I leant my tandem against a tree in the garden and we headed for the house. We said nothing until we had reached the porch. Anna was holding my hand. She spoke my name. "Fynn." It was the first word she had said for the last twenty minutes. Anna pulled her skirt and top straight and silently questioned me. I nodded. She gripped my hand tightly as we entered the sitting room.

I was a little surprised to be confronted by a man in clerical garb. He walked towards us with outstretched hand.

"Ah, John's protegé and his bright star!" He had placed his hand on Anna's head for this last remark. "John Daniel never stops talking about you!" He shook my hand once again. "Gerald Hodge."

It was many months later that I was told that Gerald Hodge was John's younger brother. It hardly seemed possible. They were so different.

Anna had wriggled away from his hand and was sitting beside me. The brothers were so different from each other that the thought of them held my attention for some minutes. Gerald had none of John's sharp cutting edge, and never spoke with those attacking sentences that I had become accustomed to. The only thing they seemed to have in common was an air of certainty.

Gerald once more placed his hand on Anna's head.

"The bright star, the bright star . . . and a little child shall lead them." I could see that she didn't really like the "bright star" stuff, but she didn't say anything. We just sat.

Gerald said, "He's told me so much about you both I feel that I know you well. He has never really loved many people, but I think he is likable." Gerald oozed goodness.

It was a week or so later that it dawned

on me that he had never used anybody's Christian name in those few hours at Random Cottage. I had been overwhelmed by his presence and had been able to say nothing more than, "How do you do?"

Though it could have been no longer than ten minutes before Arabella came into the drawing room, it seemed like hours.

"Will you go in now? He's waiting for you. I think he's a little brighter."

We started to make our way up to John's bedroom until Arabella told us that she had set up a bed for him in his study. I tapped lightly. I was relieved to hear the snap of "Well, come in, come in."

We entered, not quite knowing what to expect. John didn't look too bad, a bit washed out, perhaps. Anna had to hold his tankard of beer for him; he was none too steady.

"Not too long, I am a bit tired. I'm very glad you've come. Very. Do sit down, Fynn, for goodness sake. You make the place untidy. Sit on the bed beside me, Tich. I want to look at you."

Anna grinned and wrinkled her nose.

"Well, brat," he smiled at her, "been talking to Mister God again?"

She put her head on his shoulder and whispered to him.

"So have I Tich, so have I." I heard him say

that distinctly; there was no doubt about that.

We stayed for a few minutes longer and then I got up to leave.

"It's best," he said. "I really do want a rest."

Anna kissed him. "Goodnight, Mister John. I love you."

"I love you both. I do. You had better stay the night. You can use my bedroom. I'm not using it. You'll be alone upstairs. I don't suppose you two hunters will mind that, will you? Come and see me in the morning."

We left him.

Arabella didn't object to us staying the night, nor sleeping in John's room. Nor did she tell us not to touch anything!

Neither of us felt like sleep although we were both tired. We stood by the open window in John's room and talked.

"Fynn, Mister John loves me and you, don't he?" she said. "Yes he did, Fynn, he called me Tich. Did you hear him? And brat too."

"Did you mind?"

"No, it was nice."

We talked about little things for a while before we stretched out on the bed. Anna had her usual long conversation with Mister God, with my arm around her, and we slept. It was about midnight and I had been up since just after five that morning. Although I wanted to stay awake I couldn't. I slept.

It didn't feel as if I had had more than four hours' sleep, but I had. It felt more like four minutes. A knock at the door had shot me out of bed.

It was Arabella. "John's gone, Fynn. He's gone. About an hour ago."

So this was it, I thought. I didn't notice that Anna was beside me. She had heard it. It was odd that my first thought had been that I was glad that I was not the one to break the news to her. I was quite uncertain what came next. What to do?

Anna, in her magic way, just took over, or so it seemed. After all, seven was really a ripe old age, wasn't it?

"I'll go and make some tea," and Anna was off to do so.

It was one of those things that just happen at times. After the strain of that night the fact that Anna was off to make some tea was a bit too much for Arabella. She just exploded into peals of laughter.

"Oh, Fynn," she gasped, "she is so . . . well, what's the word, Fynn, I just don't know, she's . . ."

"She is, ain't she?" I managed to say.

True to her word, by the time we had reached the kitchen she had prepared the biggest pot of the blackest tea that she could manage.

"Done some toast for you, Fynn. Couldn't find no dripping though."

She was totally engrossed in cooking bacon and eggs for Arabella.

"I couldn't manage that. Not all that!"

No, but definitely no, Anna did not want to pay her last respects to John.

"You do, Fynn. He ain't there. He's with Mister God." And that was that.

Arabella asked us if we would mind staying with her for the day. It was Anna's suggestion that we stayed the night too.

"Why don't you let Millie come tomorrow when we've gone home?"

"Well," said Arabella, "I don't know about that." Then after a pause. "Do you think it would be all right? Would she mind? I would like some company and she could help. You telephone Mrs Bartlett and tell Millie and Doody to come."

That was the way that day progressed. We just did what we were told, whilst Anna whizzed about the kitchen producing a cup of tea every half hour or so.

It was early next morning before Millie and Doody arrived, and after they were settled in, I decided that it was time Anna and I were off.

"John left this for you, Fynn," Arabella said, handing me a letter, and some books for Anna.

On our way home I did wonder just how Arabella would make out with two young prostitutes in the house. I felt certain that John would have chuckled about it.

Millie and Doody stayed with Arabella for about a week, doing or helping to do those things that had to be done. John's body was taken up to the North of England, where his brother arranged the burial in a churchyard for which he was responsible.

Anna was absorbed by her new treasures — those books that John had left her — astronomy, mathematics, and physics. For no reason at all that I know of I didn't open John's letter to me for about two weeks. My excuse was that I had been too busy. Maybe I had been. I don't know.

"Where's John's letter, Mum?"

"Under the clock on the mantelpiece. I put it there for safety."

I opened it in the back yard. I reckoned that I wanted to be alone.

"My dear Fynn and Anna," it began, "I write to tell you what a joy it has been to know you both. You may be surprised to know that although I have had no sudden revelation or 'road to Damascus' illumination, I have at least come to the realization that I made a gross error in dismissing religion too rapidly. Now I find that it isn't the cosy hideaway I thought it to be, but hard work. Anna my dear, how right you were! I did want to know how it all started and how right you were to want to know how it all ends. Anna, if you still have that display of those circles, will you enter me at some point as a blue dot?

"My dears, I salute you and your friends.

"I salute the God-hunters. I can already hear Tich saying 'but Mister John, Mister God is hunting for us too!' I do hope so. Good luck in your searching.

"I send my love to you both.

John."

Somewhere down the line I reckon there must be an affinity between Mister John's world and Anna's, but in order to solve their problems, they had to hunt in different fields, and each saw the other's as different. Perhaps most people need both. I certainly do.

Arabella sold Random Cottage and went to live with a cousin, I think somewhere in New Zealand. Except for a few Christmas cards, that was the last I heard of her. As for Random

Cottage, it was lost, together with other houses, under a dual carriageway.

It was strange for me not to be able to share my thoughts with John any more. No more tankards of ale with him — those occasions when I spent a lot of time fending off the ice-cold logic of his attacks. Now I would have to sort out my own problems.

He had undoubtedly changed a lot during the years I had known him. Some people told me how much he had mellowed in his later years — or that he had become "almost human" after his retirement. But it wasn't that, for Old John was always very much a human — he could be hurt. Mum had told me a long time ago that the effort he had put into hiding his hurt had made him a bit irritable. Maybe she was right.

"Why do you think he caned you so often — for the fun of it?"

"I hadn't given it much thought," I replied.

"Simply to toughen you up?"

"Hold it, Mum. Hold it! I reckon I was tough enough for my age, don't you?"

"Oh, you were *strong* enough! Perhaps a bit too strong for your own good. But I don't mean that kind of strength. It's the other kind of strength I'm talking about. It was some years ago that Mister John told me that he was going to take you under his wing because you so much reminded him of himself at your age."

"I know that, Mum," I replied, "he told me that too, but I never did know what he was aiming at. I don't think that I'm anything like John."

Her eyes crinkled and she smiled. "You're more alike than you know!"

"How's that, Mum? In what ways?"

"You are just a pair of big softies!" she laughed. "And that's why he beat you so often, so that you wouldn't be too easily hurt."

"Don't know about that, Mum," I laughed. "Maybe he wasn't much to look at, but he was strong and he certainly knew how to use the old 'persuader'!"

"Oh, that," she replied, "that's nothing. You'll get a lot more hurts than that in your life. If that's the only kind of hurt you have in your life, you'll have it pretty easy."

I wasn't at all certain that I had understood her properly and said so.

"It doesn't matter," she replied. "You'll learn!"

It was just another one of those occasions when I wasn't going to get anywhere.

"He did change a lot, didn't he?" I tried another tack.

"He certainly did that, he certainly did. He was a lot more content and happier in his last two years. It was good to see it."

"It was a good thing that Anna came to live with us," I said. "I reckon she did him a power of good."

Mum looked at me a long time before she asked, "In what ways do you mean?"

"Well, all her chattering about Mister God helped him to change his mind. Don't you think so?"

She didn't answer me.

"I reckon he ended his life believing that there might be a God after all."

"Well," she replied, "he was certainly no longer convinced that there wasn't a God. That's for sure."

"I reckon he did believe," I said.

"Perhaps. All I know for sure is that the last time he came here he asked me if I could lend him a Bible."

"I'm sure Anna had a lot to do with that," I said. "She was like a . . . like a . . ."

"Don't," Mum interrupted me. "Don't say what I think you were going to say. You'll certainly be wrong."

"How do you know what I was going to say? How could you know?"

"I can read you like a book. After all, I've known you long enough. There are times I know what you're going to say before you know yourself."

"All right, then, tell me what I was going to say, if you can. Tell me!"

"A pound to a penny you were going to make the same mistake as your Aunty Doll and Mrs Weeks make, that Anna was sent by God or that she is a messenger or something like that. Come on, admit it!"

"Well," I managed, "not exactly that, but something similar, I suppose."

"Thought so!" she replied. "What a burden to hang around a child's neck! What a burden!"

"I can see that," I said, "but you've got to admit she is a bit different and I'm sure that she did help John."

"Of course she did, but not in the way you think."

"How then?"

Mum laid her hand on mine. "To use his own words, his very own words when I last saw him, 'Anna has shown me how useless it is to build Mind Mountains, and that to know God is altogether different from describing God.' I wouldn't put it that way myself . . ."

"A 'Mind Mountain'? What did he mean by that?"

"Like your stupid wall. Even if you had

leapt over it, it wouldn't have meant that you had grown up — only that you were bigger. That's a 'Mind Mountain.' So don't build any more!"

"In that case, I'll try not to. What was it about Anna? What has she got that I haven't? What did John see?"

"Well, number one, the night you brought her home you told me that she was lost, right?"

I nodded.

"If she was lost, I'm a Dutchman! Why, she's one of the few people who really knows who she belongs to, and that surely is not being lost!"

"You mean Mister God?"

I didn't need an answer to that question. I shouldn't have asked it in the first place.

"Number two," she continued, "is that she is too busy living to carry around with her any useless baggage. So don't you hang anything on to her what she doesn't need! Got me?"

"Got you, Mum."

"I reckon that just simply by her chatter and her lovingness John saw another world that he hadn't seen before — not just the world of his own knowledge. I know how much you admired him but everyone has his limits, and I'm afraid dear old John really did try to go beyond his. After he'd known Anna a bit, I think he just stopped pushing at God and then stepped back a bit."

"So what, Mum?"

"Well, I suppose you could say it gave God a chance to move forward."

"That's a difficult one for me."

"Maybe, but I have a sort of feeling that that's the way it was."

"I wish I knew why he had changed so much, Mum. I just wish I knew."

"Maybe you'll never know that." She smiled at me. "God moves in wondrous ways."

I had to be content with that.

The employees of THORNDIKE PRESS hope you have enjoyed this Large Print book. All our Large Print titles are designed for easy reading, and all our books are made to last. Other Thorndike Large Print books are available at your library, through selected bookstores, or directly from us. For more information about current and upcoming titles, please call or mail your name and address to:

THORNDIKE PRESS
PO Box 159
Thorndike, Maine 04986
800/223-6121
207/948-2962